Old King Cole

Old King Cole

A play by
Ken Campbell

**Introduced by Ken Campbell
With a foreword by FAZ**

Oberon Books
London, England

This edition published in 1989 by Oberon Books Limited
32 Russell Road, Enfield, Middlesex EN1 4TY England

First published in 1972 by Evans

Designed and typeset by O'Reilly Clark, London.
Cover design by Faz.
Printed in England by New City Printers, Edmonton, London N9
Text typeset in Garamond.

ISBN 1 870259 12 2

Oberon Books Limited

32 Russell Road, Forty Hill, Enfield, Middlesex EN1 4TY England.
Telephone: 01-367 9603 Fax: 01-363 2298

Publishing Director: James Hogan
Production Directors: Hugh O'Reilly and David Clark
Associate Editor: Nicholas Dromgoole MA (Oxon), FIChor

For
Daisy

HISTORY

Old King Cole is a pioneer of the irreverent, knockabout style of children's theatre that has become the norm since the play was first commissioned and staged by Peter Cheeseman at the Victoria Theatre, Stoke-on-Trent. Inspired by *Beano* and *Dandy*, pantomime and music-hall, this hilarious play continues to enjoy enormous success with repertory and children's theatre companies all over the country. The Old King Cole of the nursery rhyme hardly gets a look in, however, since the action is dominated by a couple of likeable villains, Faz, the dirty tricks monger, and his twitty assistant, Twoo, as they strive to wreck the wedding of Princess Daphne Cole to sporty Cyril the Fiddler. In this they are aided and abetted by an audience whose vociferous participation is guaranteed.

In his Introduction Ken Campbell explains the curious genesis of Faz and Twoo, and describes the amazing reception of the play in Stoke and elsewhere. Faz himself has contributed a characteristic Foreword.

FOREWORD (by FAZ)

When Mr. Campbell first suggested that he should turn some of my many amazing adventures into a play I was dubious. But gradually, as page by page Mr. Campbell's mammoth work neared its completion, my attitude changed from doubt to delight. Mr. Campbell had not only suceeded beyond my wildest dreams, he had created a Masterpiece. *Old King Cole* will undoubtedly take its place on the shelf of Golden Literature, somewhere in-between *Hamlet* and *Desperate Dan.* My fervent hope is that I'll be let out in time to see it performed. The Governor is optimistic.

INTRODUCTION

It began with Peter Cheeseman, artistic director of the Victoria Theatre, Stoke-on-Trent, saying that he supposed it would be all right if I wrote the kids' show that Christmas. I could write what I liked, he said, as long as the kids liked it and it was called something famous. First things first, I chased through the Oxford Book of Nursery Rhymes looking for the title. I chose Old King Cole because he was (a) a merry old soul and (b) didn't have a plot. As long as some geezer calling himself Old King Cole turned up some time or other and there was some mention of fiddlers, we'd seem to be in the clear as far as the Trades Descriptions Act was concerned.

So I thought what would you really like, kids — listen we don't want women dressed up as soppy animals do we, really? — and we don't want Magic, we've had Magic — in fact what do we really like? — the best bit is the robbers isn't it — in Panto — the funny robbers are wonderful but they always seem to cut them off short to let on the dancers — let's have funny robbers on the WHOLE TIME — that would have to be good — and I actually know a couple you'll like —

FAZ and Twoo were born on the Number 2 tour of *Fings Ain't Wot They Used T'Be* — (by Frank Norman and Lionel Bart) — and I played the part of Redhot, a brilliant creation of Norman's who wore a huge old army greatcoat and was an eighty year old kleptomaniac mutterer. On the tour, myself and actor Tony Rohr used to pass the days in jokey literary activity — we used to write novels and stuff in the following manner: he'd write one word and then I'd write the next one and so on — it wasn't exactly collaboration, since the game was to lead the narrative in ways which blew the mind of the other — one day in this manner a story opened itself in this way. "'Pass (me) me (Tony) the (me) bunsen-burner (Tony) Twoo (me)' said (Tony) Faz (me)" — and so it continued for a page or two, a somewhat garbled account of an evil genius, Faz, and his feeble-minded assistant, Twoo.

Then the whole thing started to come together in my head — now Faz and Twoo were in on the action it was certain we were well out of the Grimm and Hans Andersen inspired stuff — (jolly good stuff but anyway Hoorayyy) — and into Beano Land, Saturday Morning Pictures Captain Marvel Country — and I'd often noted how the Theatre-in-the-Round at Stoke when it didn't have any furniture on its stage looked more like a mini sports stadium than a theatre — and so I began to warm to the bravado notion of writing 'Scene 2: Wembley Stadium' — all we had to do was clear the stage and we were there — a comedy sports scene — we'd like that wouldn't we kids — ingeniously fiendish cheating — and Twoo should obviously wear the wonderful Redhot coat which I'd had the vision to nick when the *Fings* Tour packed up . . .

The first performance at Stoke was amazing — it was played to a packed audience of seven, eight and nine year olds, and they didn't just like it they went bananas — it was that great old Saturday Morning Pictures roar from beginning to end. Such was the audience response that Dave Hill (Baron Wadd) had to leave the stage for half a minute in the middle of Act Two to steel his nerve to continue the circus. Peter Cheeseman however was alarmed — he feared that the mass hysteria that the play was creating could be dangerous — so we quickly re-worked bits so they weren't quite so panic inspiring, bunged in little lulls in the action, etc. — in fact little was lost and, thanks to the Cheeseman wisdom, to my knowledge all audiences and casts have lived through the experience ever since.

It transpires that there is no German translation of the Beano, so when the very talented Wolfgang Wiens of the Theater-am-Turm in Frankfurt chanced on a script, he saw it in a way which no-one, myself included, had: as a deep political statement, mein Gott. Wiens translated it and mounted the most careful and beautiful production of it I have yet seen. I was still unable to spot the deep political meaning, but I've never been very quick on those sort of things. Faz (or Fazz as he's known in Germany, so as not to be confused with the Frankfurter Allgemeine Zeitung, a newspaper which apparently calls itself F.A.Z. for short) was performed as an incredibly accurate impersonation of Oliver Hardy, and Twoo was Stan Laurel. Anyway, it became a sensation in Germany; within two years it had achieved some sort of classic status, people writing theses and stuff on it in the Universitäts, apparently, and at the time of writing it has had over thirty different productions in the major cities of Germany and Austria.

To end on a practical note: having now seen many different productions of the piece, some with delight, some with horror, I think I can say this: it works the best, when, within its own potty Beano world, it is played as a thriller. Kids like it when you just roar through it. And you can tell. They roar back.

Ken Campbell

CHARACTERS AND SCENES

List of people you'll need for this play
THE AMAZING FAZ
Twoo (feeble-minded assistant to FAZ)
BARON WADD (weediest man in the Entire World)
SPORTS COMMENTATOR
CYRIL THE FIDDLER
OLD KING COLE
OLD QUEEN COLE
PRINCESS DAPHNE COLE

List of places you'll need
FAZ'S OFFICE
WEMBLEY SPORTS STADIUM
THE MAIN HALL OF BUCKINGHAM PALACE

The first performance of Old King Cole was given at the Victoria Theatre, Stoke-on-Trent, in December 1968 with the following cast:

FAZ	James Hayes
twoo	Terence Davies
BARON WADD	David Hill
SPORTS COMMENTATOR	James Walker
CYRIL	Shane Connaughton
OLD KING COLE	Bob French
OLD QUEEN COLE	Gillian Brown
PRINCESS DAPHNE	Jane Wood
Directed by	Peter Cheeseman and Ken Campbell
Special effects by	Richard Smerdon

Act 1

Scene The First

[The Office of the Amazing FAZ*]*

[In the office are two chairs, a large table and a hall-stand. The amazing FAZ *enters. He wears very torn trousers, odd socks, plimsolls, one spat, a striped jersey, black inverness cape and gangster hat. He is followed into the office by his feeble-minded assistant* TWOO. TWOO *wears an enormous overcoat which falls in folds on the floor.* TWOO*'s pockets don't look particularly amazing, but he seems to be able to produce almost anything you want out of them.* FAZ *is undoubtedly the finest designer and builder of traps the century has thus far produced. He is also inventor of 'Paraphernalia', a frantic, dangerous, mind-blowing activity, the equipment for which is kept in the Paraphernalia Case, a brown medium-size, tatty suitcase on which is written in bold red paint:*
PARAPHERNALIA!!!
VERY DANGEROUS!!!!!
YOU HAVE BEEN WARNED!!!!!!!
TWOO *carries the Paraphernalia Case]*

Faz The Evening Paper, please Twoo. *[The 'w' in* TWOO*'s Name is sounded as in 'twit']*

Twoo The Evening Paper, Faz?

Faz The Evening Paper, yes.

Twoo Would you rather have the Morning Paper?

Faz No.

Twoo O.

*[*TWOO *takes the evening paper out of his pocket and gives it to* FAZ. TWOO *waits for his punishment. He knows he has been naughty]*

Faz Thank you. I want to see that they've put my advertisement in all right.

Twoo O.

*[*FAZ *opens his paper and discovers the* TWOO *has cut it up and made it into a long string of dancing soldiers]*

Faz   [*In a kindly but somehow slightly sinister manner*] I see you have made my Evening Paper into a long string of dancing soldiers . . .

Twoo   Yes, Faz.

Faz   How clever.

Twoo   Clever is it, Faz?

Faz   Clever, yes. Skilful and highly ingenious.

Twoo   I thought if we painted it it would make a really good Chistmas decoration.

Faz   Yes indeed.

Twoo   You like it do you Faz?

Faz   I think it's super. There's only one thing –

Twoo   What's that Faz?

Faz   [*In a sudden fit of frantic rage, as he rips up the dancing soldiers, throwing some of the bits into the air and stuffing the rest down* TWOO*'s neck*] I hadn't read it, had I?

Twoo   No, Faz. Yes, Faz. Sorry Faz.

                 [FAZ *is still in a state. He needs a sausage to calm his nerves.* FAZ *eats sausages as if they were cigars*]

Faz   Give us a sausage, will you.

Twoo   Yes, Faz.

                 [TWOO *takes a silver case out of his pocket. He clicks it open to reveal nine nestling sausages. He takes one out and tosses it to* FAZ. FAZ *catches it in his hat*]

Faz   Ta.

                 [FAZ *takes the sausage out of his hat, taps it on the table and puts it in his mouth. He takes a little bite. He flicks the straggly bits on the carpet. The sausage seems to be calming him down*]

Faz   You're not a bad lad, Twoo. Your feeble mind is your only drawback.

Twoo   Yes, Faz.

                 [FAZ*'s eagle eye has spotted something not as it should be with his sausage*]

Faz	Errrgghhh!! What's up with this sausage?
Twoo	Where, Faz?
Faz	Look, it's got all little nibbles out of it.
Twoo	Ooo, yes.
	[TWOO *was still holding the silver sausage case.* FAZ *has now taken it from him and is inspecting the other sausages. The mystery deepens*]
Faz	They've all got little nibbles out of them.
Twoo	Ooo yes, Faz.
Faz	How's that come about?
Twoo	I don't know.
Faz	How curious.
Twoo	[*Suddenly remembering something*] Ooo Faz, last night . . .
Faz	What?
Twoo	Well I woke up in the middle of the night, last night, and I was just a little bit hungry, and I thought: 'I'll just have a sausage I think', and I did have one you see, and I must've dozed off and when I woke up this morning I saw that I'd left the lid of the sausage case open and that all the sausages had got these little marks on them which we now know to be nibbles.
Faz	Ugh! [*He spits out his sausage*] You know what that is, Twoo? You know what's done that?
Twoo	What?
Faz	A rat.
Twoo	A rat, Faz?
Faz	A rat, yes. Well he'll have to go. We'll have to get rid of him, this rat.
Twoo	Yes.
Faz	It was only our sausages last night. Tonight, what? He might be at our cakes! Nibbling our cakes!!
Twoo	Our cakes. How are we gonna get rid of him though, Faz?
Faz	By using our brains, Twoo.
Twoo	Our brains, Faz?

This is FAZ's plan of his Fantastic Sausage Baited Rat Trap

Faz	Our brains, yes. So the part you play in the exercise may be rather a small part. Ha-ha! We shall get him with cunning!
Twoo	Cunning.
Faz	And ingenuity!
Twoo	O, what you mean a trap?
Faz	Of course! A trap!! Yes. We shall build a fantastic trap. The Paraphernalia Case.

[TWOO *gets the Paraphernalia Case*]

Faz	Tie a string to handle.

[TWOO *takes a short length of string out of his pocket and ties one end to the handle of the Paraphernalia Case. Meanwhile . . .*]

Faz	[*Putting the table on its side*] Upends table.

[FAZ *goes over to the hall-stand. He picks it up, turns it upside down and leans it on a chair some distance from the table*]

Faz	Leans hall-stand on chair.
Twoo	[*Having now completed his first task*] String on handle, Faz.
Faz	Good work.

[FAZ *takes the Paraphernalia Case over to the now upended table. There happen to be two knot-holes in what is now the top of the table.* FAZ *pushes the string through one of them and pulls it through from the legs side of the table*]

Faz	Short string through Knot-hole One. [*He pulls on the string, which hoists the Case to the top*] Hoists. [*He ties it off to one of the table legs*] Makes fast.

[*Note: unless you have had several years' experience in trap building, it is unlikely that you will be able to follow what* THE AMAZING FAZ *is up to here. But you don't have to worry!* FAZ *has been kind enough to draw you a plan of this trap, which you will find on page 15*]

Twoo	I don't see how this is going to trap a rat, Faz.
Faz	Quiet, Twoo, please. I shall require another bit of string.

[TWOO *gives* FAZ *a five inch long bit of knotted string*]

Faz	[*Tossing the bit of string away*] A ball!!!!

[TWOO *takes a tennis ball out of his pocket and gives it to* FAZ. FAZ *angrily bounces the ball into the audience*]

Faz	A ball of string!!!!

[TWOO *takes a ball of string out of his pocket and gives it to* FAZ. FAZ *pokes the string through the other knot-hole*]

Faz	Long string through Knot-hole Two.

[*The ball of string is on the legs side of the table. The other end of the string* FAZ *takes over to the ball-stand and dangles it over it*]

Faz	Dangles. Sausage.
Twoo	Sausage?
Faz	Sausage, yes . . .

[TWOO *tosses* FAZ *a sausage which he catches in his hat. But during his next speech,* FAZ *gets so excited that he puts his hat back on his head*]

Faz	. . . Since our little nibbling friend is so keen on sausage, with sausage shall we bait our trap; sausage his greedy delight, sausage his ultimate downfall.
Twoo	Yes, Faz.
Faz	Let's have one then. [TWOO*'s standing there with the sausage case open. Faz helps himself to one of the sausages*]

[FAZ *ties the sausage onto the end of the string*]

Faz	Baits. Shears.
Twoo	Cheers?
Faz	Shears, yes.

[TWOO *takes a half pint of bitter out of his pocket and has a swig*]

Twoo	Cheers.
Faz	Shears!!!!!!

[TWOO *produces a large pair of garden shears*]

Twoo	Are we going to cut the grass, then Faz?
Faz	Cut the grass? No.

[*Loving it,* FAZ *snips and snaps viciously with the shears round the Paraphernalia string which is tied off to the table leg. But he doesn't actually cut through it.*

Faz	These shears will supply the final movement of this my fantastic Sausage Baited Rat Trap. [FAZ *poses against his trap*] A snap, I think, Twoo.

[TWOO *takes out his camera and points it towards* FAZ]

Faz [*Smiling triumphantly*] Cheese.

[TWOO *takes the picture.* TWOO*'s camera is a curious machine. When he pulls the lever to take the picture, there is a flash, a rude thhhppppp!!! noise, a small snow storm, and a little cuckoo who pops out to say: Cuck-oo!*]

Faz Did you get it all right?

Twoo I think so.

[FAZ *takes up another pose*]

Faz One more. Just to be on the safe side.

[TWOO *takes another photograph of* FAZ]

Camera Flash! Thhhppppp!! (Snowstorm!!!) Cuck-oo!!!!

Twoo [*Looking at the trap*] How's it work, Faz?

Faz [*Dying to*] You'd like me to demonstrate it would you?

Twoo Yes please, Faz

Faz Right. The trap is operated from here. [*He stands behind the table*] We haul in the sausage string. This string. You see. And the sausage is right outside to start with. The rat sees the sausage. About to nibble it. Then the sausage moves off. The rat doesn't know what's going on He's never seen a moving sausage before. He follows it to the hall-stand. The sausage look goes up in the air!

Twoo Tee-hee!

Faz What on earth, thinks the rat. A flying Sausage! Is it a Magic Sausage, wonders Ratty.

Twoo Tee-hee!

Faz He thinks, it's a Magic Sausage, Ratty. He's got to have it. He thinks if he gets a nibble at this Magic Sausage, he'll be granted a free wish or something.

Twoo Tee-hee!

Faz A Dancing Sausage look, it dances!! [FAZ *is yanking the string about which makes the sausage jerk about in the air*]

Twoo But it isn't really a Magic Sausage is it Faz?

Faz No. Of course it's not. It's just a Common Sausage tied on a bit of string.

Twoo	Yes.
Faz	Then we give the string a sudden yank . . . and . . .
	[FAZ *gives the string a sudden yank and the sausage leaps over the hall-stand*]
Twoo	What does Ratty do now?
Faz	He comes scampering after it, doesn't he? He wants this Magic Sausage he does. He wants his Wish.
Twoo	But he isn't going to have a Wish is he?
Faz	[*Brandishing shears dangerously*] The only wish he'll have is that he'd never seen a sausage.
Twoo	Why? What happens then?
Faz	Well look. The sausage ends up just there look. [*By the table*]
Twoo	Yes.
Faz	Under the Paraphernalia Case look.
Twoo	Yes.
Faz	Well he has a little nibble, then he sits there, having his wish, dun he?
Twoo	Yes?
Faz	Well at that moment – I won't do it now – but at that precise moment, while Ratto is down there wishing, I cut the string holding up the Paraphernalia Case and down it comes Zonk! Splonk! Klunko!!! on Ratty's head.
Twoo	Tee-hee!
Faz	Undoubtedly this will daze the rat. And while he's dazed we pick him up, take him outside and stuff him in a Pillar Box!
Twoo	Tee-hee!
Faz	Yak! Yak!
Twoo	It's a fantastic trap, Faz,
Faz	It's all right, isn't it. Let's get it hooked up.
	[FAZ *takes the sausage bait over the hall-stand and right outside. He comes back and crouches behind the table with* TWOO]
Faz	There's just one problem . . .
Twoo	What's that?

Faz	We are behind the table. How are we gonna tell when the rat starts nibbling?
Twoo	[*Looking out at the audience*] O yeah. This lot'd help you, Faz
Faz	What all these gawping herberts out here you mean?
Twoo	Yes. [*To audience*] You'll help us won't you?
Audience	Yes. Certainly. Not half. Count on me. Etc.
Twoo	Yes, they will, Faz.
Faz	[*To audience*] Well our problem is that we can't see the string from behind the table so we won't know when we've got a bite. Now when the rat bites the Sausage String will go from the Dangle Position to the Up Position. [FAZ *demonstrates*] Can you see that all right? Twoo, put a marker on the string so they can see it go up and down more easily.
Twoo	A marker, Faz?
Faz	Yes. Anything'll do. Just peg something on it.
	[TWOO *pegs an old sock on to the string as a marker*]
Faz	[*Talking to different sections of the audience*] Now when you lot here see the string go up can you signal to this lot here, and then this lot here whisper to us – you'll have to whisper or you'll frighten the rat off – whisper 'Go Sausage String'. Got that?
Audience	Seems fairly clear. I think I've almost got it. I think I know what you're after, Faz. Etc.
Faz	The rat bites the sausage. String goes to the Up Position. You lot see it. What do you do? You signal to this lot. You lot see the frantic signallings of this lot – what do you do? You whisper the order to us 'Go Sausage String'. Right. Do you lot know what to do?
First Lot	Yeahhh!
Faz	Do you lot know what to do?
Second Lot	Yeahhhh!!!!
Faz	Right to your position, Twoo.
	[FAZ *and* TWOO *take up their positions behind the table*]
Twoo	Tee-hee!

Faz	Shut up tittering, Twoo. The rat'll hear you. Suspect something's up.

[FAZ *is ready with the shears.* TWOO *is ready to wind in the sausage string*]

Faz	Are you right?
Twoo	Yes.
Faz	Are you ready?
Twoo	Yes.

[*The sausage string goes from the Dangle to the Up position, indicating that the rat is biting at the Sausage. The* FIRST LOT *of the audience spot this and signal to the* SECOND LOT, *who whisper to* FAZ *and* TWOO]

Audience	Go Sausage String!

[TWOO *gently hauls in the sausage string. Slowly the sausage starts to come on. It is followed not by a rat but by* BARON WADD, *the weediest man who ever lived*]

Baron	[*Amazed*] A moving sausage.

[*The* BARON *follows the sausage to the hall-stand. The sausage goes up in the air*]

Baron	What on earth . . . A flying sausage!

[*The sausage leaps over the hall-stand and starts to make its way to the table, followed by* BARON WADD. BARON WADD *get to the table. He stands on tip-toe to look over it*]

Faz	Here we go!!!

[FAZ *cuts the string holding up the Paraphernalia Case with his shears. The case comes thundering down on the* BARON'S *toes*]

Baron	Yiiiiiiiieeeeeee!!!!!!!!!!

[BARON WADD *capers about with the pain*]

Twoo	[*Still behind the table*] I think we got it Faz.
Faz	[*Still behind the table*] Yes. But got what?
Twoo	What?
Faz	That wasn't the noise a rat makes.
Twoo	O.

Faz	Rats don't go Yiiiiiieeee!!!
Twoo	Don't they?
	[FAZ *clouts* TWOO]
Twoo	Well what was it then?
Faz	Dunno.
	[BARON WADD *has calmed down a bit now. He hears their voices. He wanders back to the table*]
Faz	Have a Look.
Twoo	Who me?
Faz	Yes.
Twoo	Yes [*He tries to pluck up the necessary courage*] Praps it would be best if you looked, Faz.
	[FAZ *clouts* TWOO]
Faz	Have a look.
	[TWOO *stands on* FAZ's *back and peers over the table into the face of* BARON WADD]
Twoo	Hello.
Baron	Hello.
	[TWOO *pops down to report*]
Faz	What is it?
Twoo	It's a man. A very weedy one.
Faz	Ask him what his name is.
	[TWOO *pops up again*]
Twoo	Can I have you name please?
Baron	Baron Wadd.
	[TWOO *pops down to report*]
Faz	[*Not quite sure if he overheard correctly*] Who did he say he is?
Twoo	Baron Wadd.
Faz	[*Impressed, emerging from behind table*] Baron Wadd from Buckingham Palace?
Baron	Yes.

Faz	A very good evening to you, Baron.
Baron	Mr Faz?
Faz	Yes. I am Faz.
Baron	[*A great moment for him*] You are Faz.
Faz	Faz of Faz Limited, the Amazing Faz, Specialist in Traps, Disguises and Paraphernalia.
Faz & Twoo	[*Together*] Dirty Deeds Done.
	[FAZ *gives* BARON WADD *his card*]
Faz	And this is my feeble-minded assistant, Twoo.
Baron	How do you do.
Faz	Well what can we do for you, Baron? A fiendish trap?
Twoo	A fantastic disguise?
Faz	General Paraphernalia?
Baron	Well what it is, is that I've got this dirty deed that needs doing.
Faz	A low-down dirty deed?
Baron	Fairly low down, yes.
Faz	Calling for maniacal cunning and unparalleled foulness?
Baron	Well yes, it probably will, yes.
Faz	Then we are your men.
Baron	Good. Super.
	[FAZ *and* BARON WADD *shake hands.* FAZ *signals to* TWOO. TWOO *takes his camera out, and takes a photograph of them*]
Faz	Cheese. For the album, Baron.
Baron	Cheese.
Camera	Flash! Thhhpppp!! (Snowstorm!!!) Cuck-ooo!!!!
Faz	Get it all right?
Twoo	Think so.
Faz	Let's have another one just to be on the safe side. Cheese.
Baron	Cheese.
Camera	Flash! Thhhpppp!! (Snowstorm!!!) Cuck-ooo!!!!

Faz	To business.
	[FAZ *puts the table back on its legs. He sets a chair for the* BARON *and one for himself*]
Baron	There's no chance of our being overheard is there?
	[FAZ *and* TWOO *check*]
Faz	No.
Twoo	No.
Baron	What about all them?
Twoo	O they can keep a secret all right. Can't you?
Audience	'Course we can.
	[FAZ *takes off his hat and puts it on the table and scratches his head. The sausage that was in his hat is now on the table under the hat*]
Baron	The dirty deed that I require doing –
	[FAZ *puts his hat back on his head, leaving the sausage on the table*]
Baron	I say your hat has done a sausage on the table.
Faz	O goody. [*He takes a little bite out of it*] You don't mind if I Sausage?
Baron	No, carry on.
Faz	Sorry. The dirty deed, Baron. Take it slowly or my feeble-minded friend won't follow.
Baron	[*To* FAZ] Old King Cole has got one daughter.
Faz	[*To* TWOO] Old King Cole has got one daughter.
Twoo	[*To show he's heard all right*] Old King Cole has got one daughter.
Baron	Her name is Princess Daphne.
Faz	Her name is Princess Daphne.
Twoo	Her name is Princess Daphne.
Baron	Old King Cole wants her to get married.
Faz	Wants her to get married.
Twoo	Old King Cole.
Baron	And I want to marry her.

Twoo	And I want to marry her.
	[FAZ *gives* TWOO *a swipe with his hat*]
Faz	He wants to marry her.
Twoo	He wants to marry her.
Baron	Cos if I do marry Princess Daphne . . .
Faz	Cos if he do marry Princess Daphne . . .
Twoo	Cos if he do marry Princess Daphne . . .
Baron	When Old King Cole pops off, I will be King.
Faz	When old King Cole pops off –
Twoo	I will be King.
	[*Pause,* FAZ *takes off his hat ready to swipe* TWOO *with it*]
Twoo	[*Desperately to* FAZ] You'll be the King.
Faz	[*Kindly*] He'll be the King.
Twoo	[*Little voice*] He'll be the King.
	[FAZ *sits down again and puts his hat delicately back on his head*]
Twoo	[*To* FAZ] And you'll be the Queen.
	[FAZ *leaps up like lightning and swipes* TWOO *with his hat*]
Faz	No, I won't be the Queen. Princess Daphne'll be the Queen. They always get women for queens, don't they.
Twoo	O yes.
Faz	Blokes as Kings.
Twoo	Yes.
Faz	Proceed, Baron. You want to marry Princess Daphne.
Baron	But she doesn't want to marry me.
Faz	Who's she want to marry then?
Baron	She wants to marry Cyril, the King's new Fiddler.
Twoo	Fiddler?
Faz	Fiddler, yes.
Baron	Cyril the Fiddler. Old King Cole has three Royal Fiddlers
Faz	Three Royal Fiddlers.

Baron	Jonathan, Thomas and Cyril.
Faz	His fiddlers three.
Twoo	[*Still perplexed*] Fiddlers? What do they do then really these fiddlers? They just sort of stand around fiddling do they?

[TWOO *shows them what he had in mind*]

Faz	No. They fiddle on their fiddles you fool. On their violins.
Twoo	O.
Baron	Don't you know the song?
Faz	Don't you know the song?
Twoo	[*Apprehensive*] I don't think I do.

[FAZ *is about to clout* TWOO *for his appalling ignorance when he suddenly realises that he doesn't know the song either*]

Faz	What song?
Baron	I thought everyone knew it.
Faz	[*Fibbing*] Ah yes. Of course I know it . . . it's just that it's slipped my mind for the moment.
Baron	Goes like this:
	'Old King Cole was a merry old soul
	And a merry old soul was he;
	He called for his pipe and he called for his bowl
	And he called for his fiddlers three;
	Now every fiddler he had a fiddle
	And a very fine fiddle had he;
	Twee-tweedle-dee-tweedle-dee went the fiddlers –'
Twoo	Couldn't they go twoo-twoodle-doo-twoodle-doo?
Faz	[*Clouting him*] Of course they couldn't
Baron	'Merry merry men are we;
	O there's none so rare
	As can compare
	With King Cole and his fiddlers three'
	Do you think you'll remember it? Cos we have to sing it quite a bit at the Palace.
Faz	Well I shall remember it. Twoo's the problem. Do you think you're gonna remember it, little fellow?
Twoo	I think so. But I do forget things fairly quickly you know.

Faz	Go through it. Go on. See if you can go through it.
Twoo	'Old King Cool was a merry old mule And a merry old mule was Who He called for his bike and he called for his pole And he called for his tiddlers two Now every tiddler he had a tiddle And a very fine tiddle had Who Twoo-twoodle-doo-twoodle-doo went the tiddlers Very merry men go Pooh! O there's none so rare As can compare With King Cool and his cock-a-doodle-doo.'
Baron	That's not quite it.
Faz	It's as near as he'll ever get
Baron	Oh well! Back to business.
Faz	Back . . .
Twoo	. . . .to business.
	[FAZ *takes* TWOO's *hat and rubs his head in a fatherly fashion*]
Faz	Continue, Baron.
Twoo	I've forgotten what's happened so far.
Faz	[*Very fast*] Baron Wadd here wants to marry Old King Cole's daughter, Princess Daphne Cole, but she's not keen, she wants to marry Cyril the King's new fiddler. Got it?
Twoo	Yes.
Faz	Good. [*Clouts* TWOO] Baron.
Baron	Yes. Cyril's handsome you see, and good at sports, but I'm stringy and thin and my hair hangs in limp greasy wads.
Faz	Yes.
Twoo	Ugh!
Baron	I know.
Faz	But what does Old King Cole say? Does he want the Princess to marry you or Cyril?
Baron	Well Old King Cole is amazed that anyone at all wants to marry her.

Faz	Why? Isn't she very nice?
Baron	Well I suppose she's quite nice, yes, but the thing is she's silly.
Faz	[*A bit of palace gossip he hadn't heard before*] Silly!
Twoo	[*Who is falling in love with her already*] Silly is she?
Baron	Yes. At the Palace we call her Drippy Daphne.
Twoo	[*Yearningly*] Drippy Daphne . . .
Baron	Anyway Old King Cole says that whichever one of us, me or Cyril, is the best at sports, he can marry Daphne.
Faz	Best at sports. How extraordinary.
Baron	Extraordinary, Mr Faz, also unfortunate. I'm useless at sports. No good at all. My stringy legs you see. They go all funny when I run. Look, you look.
	[*The BARON shows them how he runs. He runs once round the office. He does indeed run in a very peculiar manner*]
Faz	Ugh! Yes.
Twoo	Tee-hee!
Baron	I know. And when I've got my shorts on I look really horrible.
Faz	I can imagine.
Baron	But Cyril is a top-notch sporto. His hair is sleek and kempt and he wears a watch with many dials. He's got Golden Gloves for Boxing, Silver Cups for Running, and his drawers are full of High Jump Medals. So this is where you come in Mr Faz, and you, Mr Twoo. Tomorrow in Wembley Stadium is the Big Contest. Me, Baron Wadd, versus Cyril the Fiddler. It will be your job, Mr Faz, to make sure that I win the contest. I don't care how you do it. Trap, scheme, plot or skulduggery. I leave it to you. That in short is the dirty deed I need doing. Can you do it?
Twoo	[*Explaining FAZ's pose*] He's thinking.
Faz	You will win the Big Contest, Baron.
Baron	Good.
Faz	There's just the question of our fee. What is the deal?
Baron	Well once I'm married to Princess Daphne, Faz, I'll be able to get my hands on the Royal Millions. I offer you eight hundred thousand pounds cash, Faz, if you fix it so I win Daphne.

Faz	Baron, you're on. Eight hundred thousand pounds cash, Twoo! This is our biggest job to date!!
Twoo	Yes Faz.
Baron	But nothing if you fail, cos I haven't got much money at all myself you see.
Faz	Hmmm. There's just one snag, Baron. They know me at Wembley Stadium. They know Twoo. We are notorious there. At last year's Dog Derby we entered a jet propelled greyhound, a piece of machinery of my own invention.
Baron	Did it win?
Faz	No. Unfortunately we overdid the mixture. It took off. Went into orbit. It's still up there. But there was a terrible stink about it. We were hauled before the Track Officials. No, they're bound to suspect foul play if they spot me and Twoo lurking about.
Baron	O Lord.
Faz	Just a minute! That's it! Twoo, we shall pretend to be Track Officials on the look-out for foul play. We'll pose as Track Officials – that way no-one will suspect a thing.
Baron	You mean you'll wear a disguise?
Faz	Precisely, Baron.
Baron	Fiendish. Brilliant, Faz.
Faz	[*Putting on an all-in-one disguise kit of nose, glasses, moustache and eyebrows*] Disguise number forty-eight will serve our purpose, Twoo.
	[TWOO *puts his forty-eight on*]
Baron	A fiendish disguise, Faz.
Faz	It's not finished yet. Disguise accessories eighteen and thirty-four.
	[TWOO *produces two squashed flat opera hats. He gives one to* FAZ *Faz knocks open his hat.* TWOO *has trouble with his.* FAZ *does it for him.* FAZ *produces a cane suddenly. Note: Use spring steel 'magic' expanding canes*]
Baron	Fiendish

[TWOO *is clicking the fingers of his right hand trying to produce a magic cane like* FAZ *did. Suddenly one produces itself in his left hand, which makes him jump. They both take off their hats and produce bunches of flowers out of them, which they put in their buttonholes*]

Baron   Fantastic.

Faz   [*Gesturing to* TWOO *that a snap is called for*] Twoo. Baron. Cheese

Baron   Cheese.

Camera   Flash! Thhpp!! (Snowstorm!!!) Cuck-ooo!!!!

Faz   Get it all right?

Twoo   I think so.

Faz   One more just to be on the safe side. Cheese.

Baron   Cheese.

Camera   Flash! Thhpp!! (Snowstorm!!!) Cuck-ooo!!!

Faz   The Paraphernalia Case, Twoo.

                     [TWOO *goes and picks up the Paraphernalia Case*]

Baron   Do you think you may have to resort to Paraphernalia then, Faz?

Faz   Always best to be prepared, Baron. Right!

Faz, Twoo & Baron
                     [*Together*] To Wembley Stadium!!

                     [*And off they go. But see Appendix I*]

Scene The Second

[*Wembley Sports Stadium*]

[*The* MASTER OF CEREMONIES *steps into the arena. He uses a microphone*]

MC   My Lords, Ladies and Gentlemen, welcome to Wembley Sports Stadium for another afternoon of assorted sport. We have an especially exciting Contest here for you today: A Special Nine Round Royal Challenge Match between Baron Wadd and Cyril the Fiddler. In the snazzy, bri-nylon track suit – Cyril the Fiddler!

[CYRIL THE FIDDLER, *kitted in Olympic track suit, trots into the arena.*
He waves to the crowds]

MC   And in the brown, egg-stained dressing-grown – Baron Wadd!

[BARON WADD *in his old dressing-gown steps into the arena, followed*
by FAZ *and* TWOO *int their Track Official disguises.* FAZ *holds the*
baron's weedy arm high in the air, as if presenting a future World
Champion]

MC   And the winner of this Contest will be offered the hand
in marriage of Princess Daphne. In a very few minutes His
Majesty Old King Cole, Her Majesty Old Queen Cole, and Her
Royal Highness Princess Daphne Cole will be entering the
Royal Enclosure here at Wembley. As is usual as soon as I see
the Royal Party coming I shall ask you all to stand.

Old Queen Cole's voice
Don't be so silly, Daphne.

MC   Here come the Royal Party now.

[*Enter* OLD KING COLE, OLD QUEEN COLE *and* PRINCESS DAPHNE COLE]

MC   My Lord, Ladies and Gentlemen, please be upstanding for His
Majesty the King.

Old King Cole   Please sit down everybody.

[*As the audience sits down again,* DAPHNE *waves to them in a most*
unprincess-like way]

Daphne   Yoooooooo-hoooooo everybody! Thhhhhpp!!

Queen   Don't be so silly Daphne. Behave yourself.

[*Daphne puts her hands to her head and waggles them in an*
exceptionally rude way]

Queen   Daphne!

[DAPHNE *takes up a position of strained good.* TWOO *has fallen in*
love with her]

King   Let the Contest begin.

MC   The contest will consist of the best of nine events. Which
are: Boxing, Egg and Spoon Race, Sword Fighting, Shooting,
Archery, High Jump, Long Jump, Fire Diving and Pole Vault. So
first on the agenda: The Boxing Match. On my right at twelve
stone eight pounds, in the smartly pressed white trunks –
Cyril the Fiddler!

[CYRIL *instantly unrobes to reveal his immaculate strip*]

The Crowd   Boooooooooo!

MC   On my left at a weedy seven stone, in the Army Surplus droopy drawers is Baron Wadd!

[*The* BARON *drops his dressing-gown to reveal his pathetic physique and laughable kit*]

Crowd   [*Surprisingly*] Hooooooorayyyy!

[FAZ *and* TWOO *were encouraging the crowd to cheer the* BARON. *The* KING *wonders who they are*]

King   Baron!

Baron   Yes your Majesty?

King   Who on earth are those two?

Baron   These two?

King   Yes.

Baron   Er –

Faz   [*Bounding in*] We're Track Officials, your Majesty. We're here to make sure there's no foul play.

Baron   Heh! Heh!

King   Splendid.

Faz   An honour, your Majesty. [*He signals to* TWOO *to get his camera out*] Cheese! See if you can get the Whole Royal Party in.

The Royal Party Cheese!

Camera   Flash! Thhhpppp!! (Snowstorm!!!) Cuck-oo!!!

King   You'll let us have a copy if it comes out?

Faz   Of course.

Twoo   [*Who has taken out his photo orders note book. To the* KING] Name and address?

Faz   The King, Buckingham Palace, you fool! [*Clouts* TWOO]

Twoo   O yes.

Cyril   [*To* MC] Would you help me with my Golden Gloves, please?

MC   Certainly.

[MC *helps* CYRIL *to tie up the laces of his Golden Boxing Gloves. Meanwhile . . .*]

Baron   What's the plan for the Boxing, Faz?

Faz   Twoo, the special gloves for the Baron. [TWOO *produces a biggish heavy-looking pair of gloves*] They're full of iron and lead and other very heavy metals. One sock from one of these and he'll be spark out.

Baron   Fiendish! [FAZ *hold the gloves and the* BARON *slips his hands in*]

[*The* MC *has now finished helping* CYRIL. *He's back at the microphone*]

MC   [*For the benefit of the listeners at home*] The Track Official is helping the Baron on with his gloves. Meanwhile Cyril the Fiddler gracefully limbers his rippling muscles. Contestants as soon as you're ready please! One of the Track Officials has wandered over to the Royal Party. He seems to be saying something to the Princess. But I can't quite make out what it is . . .

Twoo   [*To* DAPHNE] Hello.

Daphne   Hello.

[*Coyly and shyly they play about with each other like two little kids touching and prodding at each other*]

Queen   All right Daphne. That's enough. Don't get over-excited Daphne, will you stop playing with the Official. [*To* TWOO] Shooo!

[TWOO *returns to* FAZ *and the* BARON. FAZ *is still holding up the* BARON'*s gloves so that the great weight of the gloves doesn't strain his weedy arms*]

MC   [*In the centre of the ring*] Contestants please.

[*The* BARON, *his gloves still supported by* FAZ, *enters the ring, where he meets* CYRIL. *The* MC *says some private words to the contestants*]

MC   A one round contest. One Knockout of a count of ten to decide the winner. Seconds out.

Gong   Bong!

[FAZ *and* TWOO *leave the ring. As soon as* FAZ *lets go of the* BARON'*s gloves the weight of them pulls him to the floor*]

MC	[*Commentating*] . . . And the Baron is on the floor right away . . . He's trying to heave himself up . . . but some unseen, invisible force seems to be holding his glove to the floor . . . Meanwhile Cyril satisfies himself with a left then a right, then a beautiful left hook there to the Baron's hindquarters . . . the Baron now straining to get up . . . he makes an almighty effort . . . and yes, he's now on his feet . . . but he's staggering about, his muscles, which have been described as being like baby sparrow's knee-caps, seemingly quite out of control . . . he's fallen now into the arms of the Track Officials . . . the Track Officials swing him back into the fray . . . one of the Baron's swinging gloves strikes Cyril a blow! . . . Cyril falls!!! What an extraordinary turn of events. [*He leaps into ring to count* CYRIL *out*] One. Two. Three. [CYRIL *gets up*] But Cyril is on his feet again after a count of three. The crowd here at Wembley going mad with excitement . . . Cyril, all time Olympic Champion, knocked down for a count of three, by Baron Wadd, who experts claim is in fact the weediest man in the entire world . . . but the effort of the blow seems to have sapped the remainder of the Baron's almost non-existent strength . . . the Baron looking very groggy as Cyril moves in . . . a vicious left, by Cyril . . . a right to the body . . . a left to the jaw . . . the Baron falls against Cyril . . . Cyril appearing to hold the Baron up in a clinch . . . the Baron coming in for an immense amount of punishment from this great figure of the fighting world, Cyril the Fiddler . . . but the baron, encouraged by the Track Officials, takes a swing at the back of Cyril's right leg . . . Cyril's leg give way . . . it only appeared to be a puny swing by the Baron from where I am . . . but Cyril's down on his knee . . . the Baron tries to take a swipe at Cyril's jaw . . . but Cyril ducks and the Baron goes over backwards . . . The Baron is on the floor . . . he seems unable to get up . . . Cyril hops over to be ready in case the Baron manages to get up . . . The Track Officials fanning the Baron with their towels . . . but I think it's all in vain . . . [*Leaping in to count him out*] four – five – six – seven – eight – nine – ten – OUT!!
Bell	Ting a ling ling ling!
MC	The Winner by a knockout in the first round . . . Handsome Cyril the Fiddler!!
Crowd	Boooooooh!
MC	And a hand for the loser, weedy Baron Wadd!

Crowd	Hoooooorayyyyy!!
MC	The Score – one nil to Cyril!

[*The Mechanical Scorer Clocks up the Score:*
                    CYRIL   BARON
                        1   0   ]

Baron	It was a fiendish scheme, Faz, but it was foiled because you didn't realise quite how weedy I am.
Faz	No, I certainly didn't realise you were this weedy.
Baron	I know. I am incredibly weedy you see.
Faz	Yes.
Baron	What is the plan for the egg and spoon race, Faz?
Faz	Twoo, show the Baron the special egg and spoon we have prepared for him.

[TWOO *produces an egg on a spoon*]

Baron	But that just looks like an ordinary egg on an ordinary spoon.
Faz	Precisely Baron. It LOOKS like an ordinary egg on an ordinary spoon. Now in the egg and spoon race you have to race round the track balancing an egg on a spoon . . .
Baron	Yes I know.
Faz	And that's the difficult bit, trying to keep it on the spoon.

[FAZ *demonstrates how difficult it is. It is amazing the way he just manages to keep the egg on the spoon*]

Baron	Watch out! . . . You'll . . . [FAZ *holds the egg and spoon over the* BARON*'s head. He twists it over but the egg doesn't leave the spoon*] Watch out! Don't be a fool, Faz! . . . Good Lord!
Faz	We have Sellotaped the egg to the spoon.
Twoo	With Sellotape.

[FAZ *suddenly scared that they might be overheard disappears the egg and spoon into* TWOO*'s overcoat. He and the* BARON *retire out of the way*]

MC	The contestants just cooling down before the next gruelling event . . . the Egg and Spoon Race . . . the crowd seem to have settled down after the excitement of the Boxing Match . . . the Queen seems to be enjoying a private joke with the King . . .

[*The* KING *and* QUEEN *having a little laugh. They are interrupted by* DAPHNE]

Daphne Can I have an ice cream, Mum?

Queen You've already had eighteen today.

Daphne O go on, Mum. Let me have an ice cream.

Queen Don't be so silly, Daphne. If you're going to be silly you'll have to go back to the Palace.

Daphne O Mum! I've got to stay. I've got to see who I've got to marry, haven't I?

Queen Well if you want to stay, just don't act so silly.

Daphne I wasn't acting silly. I just wanted an ice cream.

Queen That'll do, Daphne. I don't want to hear any more about it.

[*The* QUEEN *haughtily reads her sports programme and ignores Daphne.* TWOO *has overheard all this. He goes to* DAPHNE. *He takes an ice cream out of his pocket and gives it to her. He dashes back to* FAZ]

Daphne [*To* TWOO, *as he races off*] I think you're super.

Queen Daphne, where did you get that ice cream from?

Daphne The Track Official. He happened to have one in his pocket.

Queen Don't be so silly Daphne. Track Officials don't carry ice creams around in their pockets.

Daphne [*To audience*] Well that one does, doesn't he?

Crowd Yeaaaah!

Queen [*Waves graciously at her people. Then turns crossly to her daughter*] Well you're not to have any more after that one.

MC The Egg and Spoon Race . . . [*He sets down eggs and spoons on the start line of the running track*] . . . Contestants please.

Baron But how will you swap the fiendish egg and spoon for that real egg and spoon?

Faz Leave that to us, Baron. Shhh!

MC Cyril, can you stand here please, behind this egg and spoon, and you behind this one, Baron.

[BARON *looks to* FAZ *for reassurance*]

MC	[*Talking very fast*] Now I shall give you 'One – two – three – Go!' On the word 'Go!' you will pick up your egg and spoon and race twice round the track; if you drop your egg you may pick it up again but you musn't use your hands, only your spoon. But if your egg breaks you are automatically disqualified and out of the race. Do you understand the Rules?
Cyril	Perfectly.
Baron	I think so.
MC	Right. Are you ready, contestants?
Cyril	Absolutely.
Baron	I don't know.
MC	One – two – three – G – . . .
	[FAZ *and* TWOO *leap onto the track and stop the race*]
Faz	Objection!
Twoo	FOWL!
Faz	Offside!
MC	What's the matter?
Queen	What's going on?
King	An obection from the Track Official.
	[FAZ *and* TWOO *have been bent down inspecting the* BARON's *egg*]
Faz	Objection sustained!
MC	What is the objection?
Faz	Harry Wobblers! I saw that egg wobble! I think it may be about to hatch.
King	The egg's about to hatch!
Faz	Into a chicken! Stethoscope, please!
	[TWOO *gives* FAZ *a stethoscope.* FAZ *listens in to the* BARON's *egg*]
MC	[*Commentating*] What a tense moment as the Track Official makes a medical examination of the egg . . . he listens first to the large end . . . and then to the little end . . . Yes . . . I think he's reached a decision . . .
Faz	Yes, if my diagnosis is correct this egg will be having a happy event very shortly.
MC	Good Lord!

King	A good job these Track Official chappies turned up, eh, Brenda?
Queen	Yes indeed, Charlie.
MC	[*Picking up the egg very carefully*] I'll take this back and get another. Fortunately, there are another four in the box.
Faz	No need to bother. My feeble-minded friend here happens to have an egg on him.
MC	O good.
	[MC *runs off carefully with the egg.* FAZ *and* TWOO *watch him go and then* TWOO *takes out the fiendish egg and spoon and puts it down. He snaffles the other spoon into his pocket, while* FAZ *diverts* CYRIL's *attention*]
Faz	[*Pointing vigorously to the sky for* CYRIL's *benefit*] Look, a lesser-spotted doobry!
Cyril	Where?
Faz	Watch out! [*He shields* CYRIL's *head with his cape*]
	[*While no-one seems to be looking, the* BARON *can't resist having a little play with the fiendish egg and spoon*]
Baron	Heh! Heh!
MC	[*Returning suddenly*] Ah good are we ready?
	[*The* BARON *is startled. In his panic he puts the egg and spoon down on* CYRIL's *side*]
Cyril	Absolutely. [*To* FAZ] Thank you.
Faz	My pleasure.
MC	One – two – three –Go!
	[*Cyril and the* BARON *pick up the eggs and spoons and race off. Cyril has got the fiendish egg and spoon, so he completes his two laps in no time. The* BARON's *egg goes shooting off the end of his spoon, high into the air and into the audience. Note: Use a 'blown' egg if the audience aren't in dungarees*]
MC	[*Commentating*] Cyril off to a very good start there!... What an example of that 'go' which puts the Great in Great Britain... Hello, the Baron in trouble... his egg is going right up in the air... and panic as it comes down right in the middle of the crowd here at Wembley... and Cyril flies in for a dazzling first place.

Baron	Bah!
MC	Winner of the Egg and Spoon Race, Wembley's darling, Cyril the Fiddler!
Crowd	Booooooh!
MC	And a hand for the loser, weedy Baron Spindle-shanks Wadd!
Crowd	Hooooooooorayyyy!!

[*The Royal Party are equipped with Royal Football Rattles and Royal Silly Noise Hooters, which they seem to enjoy using enormously*]

MC	The Score now stands at Cyril two, Baron, nil. The next event will be the Sword Fighting.

[*The Mechanical Scorer:*
         CYRIL   *BARON*
           2   0   ]

King	Ah good. The Sword Fighting now, Brenda.
Queen	Mmmmmmmmmm.
Faz	Don't worry Baron, you could still win 7-2.
Baron	What's the plan for the sword fighting?
Faz	It can't fail. We've fixed one of the swords. One of the swords is useless. The other one is all right. All you've got to do is make sure you get the All Right Sword.
Baron	How do I know which is which?
Faz	The blue sword is the one you want. The useless sword has got a little ball on the handle – a pom pom. You don't want that one.
Baron	So I want the one with the little ball?
Faz	The blue one.
Baron	The one with the blue ball.
Faz	No. Just remember this: The sword that is blue is the sword that is true; the sword with the ball is no good at all.
Baron	The sword that is blue is the sword that is true; The sword with the ball is no good at all.
Faz	Again!

Faz, Twoo & Baron

[*Together. To drum it into the* BARON's *panicky mind they do it very rythmically.* TWOO *starts to dance.* DAPHNE *sees him dancing and leaves the Royal Enclosure to go and dance with him. Meanwhile* CYRIL *is donning his fencing gear*] The sword that is blue is the sword that is true; The sword with the ball is no good at all. The sword that is blue is the sword that is true; The sword with the ball is no good at all.

[*The* QUEEN *suddenly notices the dancing*]

Queen Daphne, stop that dancing now!

MC [*Commentating*] A humourous little event. Her Majesty the Queen has suddenly spotted her daughter jiving on the turf with a Track Official. And she's calling to the Princess to come back.

Queen Daphne! Stop dancing now! O do something, Charlie!

King Stop dancing now!

MC The King now called in to assist!

[*The* QUEEN *drags her away, slapping her legs.* TWOO *goes back to* FAZ. FAZ *was too busy with the* BARON *to notice any of this*]

Daphne O Mum! What was I doing?

Queen You were making a silly exhibition of yourself with the Track Official.

Daphne O I wasn't Mum. I was just dancing with him. Not allowed to dance now.

Queen Quiet, Daphne. I don't want to hear any more about it.

Daphne But Muuuum . . .

Queen Quiet, Daphne. Sit still.

King There's a good girl.

[MC *brings on the two swords. One is blue. One has a ball on the hilt. The one with ball is in a white scabbard*]

MC The Sword Fighting contest. Baron Wadd, would you like to choose a sword please.

Baron Thank you my man . . . I would like the one with the blue – I beg your ball – the one with the pardon. O panic ! [*He whispers to* FAZ] What is it?

Faz & Twoo	[*Together, whispering vigorously*] The sword that is blue is the sword that is true; The sword with the ball is no good at all.
Baron	O yes. [*To* MC] I would like the er . . . The sword that is ball is the sword that is tall; The sword that is white is the . . . White?!? There's three swords! O no. Sorry! The sword that is white gave me a fright!
King	Hoy Baron! Get on with choosing your sword. This is a Sports Meeting man. Not a Poems Festival.
Baron	Yes your Majesty! Justaminutejustaminute!
Faz	[*Exhorting the Wembley crowd*] Blue, tell him! Blue!
Baron	[*Not seeming to hear the crowd*] The sword that is blue is blooming no good to you – so . . . I'll have the one with the ball.
	[*He takes the sword with the ball*] The sword with the ball is the best of all.
	[FAZ *expires with frustration*]
MC	Yours is the blue sword then, Cyril.
Cyril	Thank you.
MC	I shall give you 'One – two – three – Go!' and on the word 'Go' you will draw swords and with a cry of 'En garde' set about each other. Do you understand?
Cyril	Perfectly.
Baron	I think so.
MC	Are you ready?
Cyril	Absolutely
Baron	More or less.
MC	One – two – three – Go!
Baron & Cyril	[*Drawing swords*] En garde!
	[CYRIL's *sword is super. He flashes around with it. The* BARON's *sword is bendy and useless. Ridiculous sword fight*]
MC	[*Commentating*] . . . Cyril off to a flying start . . . his vorpal blade snicking and snacking round the Baron's head and body like a bandersnatch! . . . the Baron as yet making only feeble parries to Cyril's constant swipes and swishes . . . The

Baron seems to be having trouble with his sword . . . his sword is drooping to the floor . . . he's making a run for it . . . the Baron is running away! . . . He's imploring the crowd at Wembley to hide him from Cyril . . . Cyril standing his ground in the Arena, challenging the Baron to return to the fray . . . Cyril boldly puts his sword on the ground and stands with his arms folded . . . Now a Track Official's given it to the Baron . . . th Baron now climbs back into the Arena with two swords . . . he's lunging at Cyril with both his swords . . . Cyril definitely worried . . . listen to the roar of the crowd here at Wembley while they watch one of the most incredible events of the decade . . . Gosh! . . . O no . . . good Lord! . . . Gosh! . . . Ooooo! . . . O no . . . O . . . In an incredible fashion, dodging and darting this way and that, Cyril has broken past both the Baron's swords . . . and he's taken one of the swords off the Baron, and with startling efficiency he forces a total submission from the Baron. The Baron pleading for his life.

[FAZ *throws in the towel*]

MC	Winner of the Sword Fighting: sleek, kempt, pleasant-smelling Cyril the Fiddler!
Crowd	Booooooh!
MC	And a hand for the loser, waddy-haired Baron Stinky Wadd!
Crowd	Hooooorayyy!!
Baron	Bah! Foiled again!
MC	The Score now stands at Cyril three, Baron nil. The next event will be the Shooting. I'll go and get the rifles.

[*The Mechanical Scorer changes to:*
         CYRIL   *BARON*
           3   0   ]

Baron	Things are desperate, Faz.
Faz	If you win everything else you could still win 6-3. The Shooting is in the bag.
Baron	What happens?
Faz	Well what you've got to do is shoot a duck isn't it?
Baron	Yes.
Faz	Well Twoo's got a duck in his pocket.

Twoo	I've got a duck in me pocket.
Faz	So you just fire off anywhere and Twoo slings his duck in as if it's fallen out the sky; and when it's Cyril's turn, Twoo'll creep round behind him, posing as a cameraman, and just as he's about to fire – he'll yank his shorts down.
Baron	Fiendish! That really is fiendish, Faz!
MC	[*Commentating*] The contestants just having a breather before the Shooting, which will be starting in approximately one minute. O just a minute . . . Cyril seems to be waving at me . . . Yes Cyril?
Cyril	One minute seventeen point four seconds if you want to be exact!
MC	Ah! Cyril, having consulted his underwater, multi-dialled, Brylcream Boy of the Month Watch informing me of the absolutely, exact time till the Shooting Contest . . . Wonderful character Cyril . . . wonderful, wonderful chap . . . [*Sort of to himself*] Dunno why I find him such a pain . . . Princesss Daphne seems to be trying to get her Mother's attention in the Royal Enclosure.
Daphne	Er, Mum?
Queen	Yes, Daphne?
Daphne	This thought, you see, suddenly came to me, and it was such a beautiful thought that it can only have come from the Angels. Would it, I thought, be nice if we all had a lollipop now?
Queen	No you're not going to have a lollipop, Daphne.
Daphne	No I didn't jst mean me, I meant you and Dad as well, all of us – we could ALL have a lolly.
Queen	No, Daphne. Apart from the fact that it would spoil your dinner, lollipops are filthy things. They're made by filthy old women in dirty scummy kitchens who don't use handkerchieves. They're germy, filthy things, lollipops.
Daphne	O go on, Mum. I could flit it before I eat it. I could spray it with disinfectant and DDT – that'd kill the germs.
Queen	Quiet, Daphne. I don't want to hear any more about it.

[*The Queen goes all haughty and reads her sports programme.* TWOO *slinks over to* DAPHNE. *He produces a lollipop and a flit gun for her.* FAZ *notices that* TWOO *has strayed.* DAPHNE *flits her lolly*]

Faz	[*Calling him back*] Twoo!
	[TWOO *goes back to* FAZ]
Queen	[*Getting sprayed by* DAPHNE'S *flit*] Daphne! What're you doing? How dare you flit me.
Daphne	Sorry, Mum. I was flitting my lolly.
Queen	Where did you get that lollipop and flit gun from?
Daphne	That Track Official happened to have them in his pocket.
Queen	Don't be so silly, Daphne. A Track Official wouldn't have lollipops and flit guns in his pockets.
Daphne	[*To audience*] Well that one does, doesn't he?
Crowd	Yeeessss!
	[DAPHNE *licks her lollipop. She makes a nasty face*]
Daphne	Err Mum . . .
Queen	What?
Daphne	It doesn't taste very nice this lollipop.
Queen	I'm not surprised. I'm not at all surprised it doesn't taste very nice if you've just flitted it. It serves you right Daphne. It just serves you right for your silliness.
	[*Pause*]
Daphne	Mum?
Queen	What?
Daphne	I'm going to have to spit.
Queen	O no. Charlie?
King	What?
Queen	Daphne says she's going to have to spit.
King	O Lord! Can't you wait till we get back to the Palace, Daphne?
	[DAPHNE *stamps her foot and shakes her head*]
Queen	Have you got anything for her to spit in?
King	[*Hunting and rummaging*] O Lord! I don't know. I don't think so. No. O Lord! You are a pest Daphne.
	[TWOO *trots over and produces a metal cup*]

Queen	O look Charlie, that extraordinary Track Official has come across with a metal cup for Daphne to spit into.
King	O good. Thank you very much.
	[DAPHNE *dribbles into the cup. She hands* TWOO *back the lollipop*]
Twoo	Don't you want it then?
Daphne	No, because it doesn't taste very nice.
	[TWOO *produces another one.* DAPHNE *takes it. The* QUEEN *sees this time.* TWOO *nips back to where* FAZ *is*]
Daphne	See he's got everything, that Track Official. Could I marry that funny Track Official, Mum, do you think, instead of Cyril or that horrible Baron?
Queen	Don't be silly, Daphne.
Daphne	But everything I ever want is in his pockets.
Queen	Quiet, Daphne.
MC	[*Bringing on rifles*] Contestants for the Shooting Contest to the centre of the Arena, please.
Baron	So I fire anywhere and Twoo tosses in a duck?
Faz	That's it! Shhh!
MC	Right. The Shooting Contest. Would you like to choose a rifle, Cyril.
Cyril	Anyone'll do. It's what you do with it that counts. [*He takes one*] Thank you.
MC	Baron. [*He gives him the other rifle*]
Baron	Thank you. [*The* BARON *looks frightened of it already*]
MC	Now you know the rules don't you. Yow will each have one shot and one shot only, with which you must shoot a duck flying overhead. Do you understand?
Cyril	Perfectly.
Baron	I think so.
MC	Would you like to shoot first, Baron?
Baron	[*To* FAZ] Would I?
Faz	[*Bawling*] Yesss!
Baron	[*Bawling*] Yesss!!

[*The* MC *jumps, startled by the* BARON *shouting 'Yeeess' in his ear*]

MC   Baron Wadd will fire first. In your own time, Baron.

          [*The* BARON *loads his rifle. He puts it to his shoulder. He is very
          scared. He shuts his eyes. He just can't quite pluck up enough
          courage to squeeze the trigger. But his body starts to squeeze up,
          which means that the gun instead of pointing up in the air is
          pointing at the Royal Family*]

MC   [*Commentating*] The Baron puts the rifle to his shoulder . . . he
          doesn't look very happy . . . I'm not quite clear whether he's
          seen a duck or not yet . . . I rather think not as his eyes appear
          to be tight closed . . . an expectant hush from the tensed
          crowd here at Wembley . . . The Baron's body seems to be
          crumpling up . . . and Good Lord . . . I don't believe it . . .

King   Get down Brenda! On the floor woman! Daphne get down . . .

MC   The Baron is pointing his gun at the Royal Family!!

Faz   Point the thing in the air, Baron! Baron!

MC   Track Official warning the Baron . . . the Baron's swinging the
          gun away . . . but it's now pointing at the Track Officials!!!

Faz   Get down Twoo!! [*He leaps Commando-like on to his stomach*]

King   All clear I think now, Brenda.

MC   And now the gun is menacing the crowd!

          [*The* BARON *in his terror is now unconsciously pointing the gun at
          the audience*]

MC   Get down! Get down behind your seats, kids! Take cover!
          Down behind your seats!! The crowd in a great panic diving
          for cover behind their seats . . . some are praying . . . some are
          yelling at this lunatic . . . the gun moving off the crowd and
          pointing at the floor.

          [*The* BARON, *his eyes still tight shut, fires at the floor*]

Gun   Bang!

MC   And the Baron has fired at the floor.

Faz   [*Excitedly gesturing towards the sky*] He's got one! It's a hit! He's
          got one! He's bagged a duck look!

King   What do you mean he got one? He fired at the floor, man.

Faz	No! The bullet must've bounced! How fantastic! It must've bounced on the floor and gone right up in the air and got that duck.
MC	What duck?
Cyril	I can't see a duck and I've got incredibly good eyesight.
	[*Everyone is looking up in the air*]
Faz	[*Frantic*] Up there look! Here it comes now! Hurry up Twoo! Wheeeeeeeeeeee!
	[TWOO *tosses in a rubber bath-time squeaking duck*]
Faz	Congratulations Baron! [*He suddenly sees the duck clearly*] Twoo, that's a toy one!
Twoo	Is it?
Faz	Is it? Of course it is. It's a rubber bath-time squeaking duck.
	[*Grabbing the Baron's hand to divert attention*] Well done, Baron.
King	I say there, Track Official!
Faz	Yes, your Majesty?
King	That's a funny looking duck, isn't it?
Faz	That don't matter, your Majesty.
King	What do you mean 'It don't matter'?
Faz	The rules say any duck counts – whether it's funny looking or serious looking. Isn't that right?
MC	It's a tricky point! The only case which compares in any way with this was the Phil Gooblet affair in 1934. Gooblet, while attempting to shoot a duck, shot down a helicopter. The Judges awarded him a second prize which he sportingly gave to the Pilot's widow. Shall we give the Baron another shot?
King	O no. I can't go through all that again.
MC	Well, perhaps the fairest thing would be to put it to the vote, your Majesty?
King	Yes. That's a good idea. Yes.
MC	[*Addressing the crowd*] Well now, if you think the Baron's rubber bath-time squeaking duck should count, will you please raise your right hands now. This is if you think it SHOULD count.

[FAZ, TWOO and the BARON encourage the crowd to raise their hands. The MC, helped by FAZ and TWOO, count the hands]

MC   And now would you raise your right hands if you think that the Baron's duck definitely SHOULD NOT count. Thank you. Well your Majesty, by an overwhelming majority the Baron's rubber bath-time squeaking duck does count!

The Crowd   Hoooorayyyy!

[FAZ, TWOO and the BARON celebrate wildly]

MC   Right. Now Cyril the Fidler's turn to fire. In your own time, Cyril.

[Into microphone] Can we have complete quiet please, while Cyril squeezes his trigger.

Cyril   Thank you.

[CYRIL loads his rifle. He puts it to his shoulder to take aim. In a moment TWOO will creep up behind him, posing as a cameraman]

MC   *[Commentating]* Cyril . . . his rifle at the ready . . . Yes! I think he's seen something . . . he's looking into the distance . . . I think he's onto a duck . . . I can't see a thing but I've only got normal sight . . . Cyril of course has got incredibly good eyesight . . . good eyesight, good looks, great sportsman, wonderful musician, always clean and neat . . . his rugged profile thrust towards the sky . . . he's being pursued rather closely by a strange looking cameraman . . . Yes! He's definitely seen a duck . . . I think he's about to fire.

[TWOO pulls down CYRIL's shorts revealing the fact that under them CYRIL wears red pants. CYRIL is put off his stroke completely and in his confusion fires at FAZ's large bottom. FAZ leaps a couple of yards into the air and grabbing at his bottom hares round the track]

Faz   Water! Water!

[TWOO races out to get some water]

Daphne   Red pants! Cyril wears red pants!

MC   *[Commentating]* The Track Official has suddenly gone chasing off round the track. His face was very red and he seemed to be in very great pain as he leapt up in the air and went charging off. It could very well be a lap record.

Faz   Water, Twoooooo!

[TWOO *comes trotting in with a bucket of water. He puts it down.* FAZ *sits in it*]

Faz	Phorrrr! That's better.
MC	The result of the Shooting – what was the result of the Shooting?
Faz	The result of the Shooting was – I was shot IN THE BOT!!!!
Daphne	Cyril wears red pants!
Queen	That'll do Daphne.
MC	The score now stands at Cyril three, Baron one.
Crowd	Hoooorayyy!

[*The Mechanical Scorer changes to:*
        CYRIL   BARON
          3   1   ]

MC	The next match will be the Archery. I'll go and get the bows and arrows.
Faz	You've won then, Baron! But at what a cost!
Baron	Right. How does the Archery go then, Faz?
Faz	[*Still sitting in his bucket*] You just twang off in any direction, Baron. Twoo's got a spare arrow – he'll stick it in the target and he'll say . . . What're you going to say, Twoo?
Twoo	'Oo look the Baron's scored a bull'.
Baron	Well that sounds fairly fiendish.
Faz	Yes well, we'll see.
Daphne	Mum?
Queen	Yes?
Daphne	No chance of a Swiss Roll?

[TWOO *throws* DAPHNE *a whole Swiss Roll*]

Queen	Where did you get that?
Daphne	Track Official. [*To* CROWD] Did, didn't he?
Crowd	Yeesss!
Daphne	And I want to marry him.
Queen	Daphne you will marry whoever wins the Big Sporting Contest, because that is the wish of your father.

Daphne	Do you know what I'm going to give you for Christmas?
Queen	No. What Daphne?
Daphne	[*Very rudely*] A gobstopper.
Queen	Daphne that's it! You're going back to the Palace.

[*The* QUEEN *tries to drag* DAPHNE *home. But* DAPHNE *won't come*]

Daphne	O no! Mum! Mum! No! I'm sorry . . . I didn't mean to be rude . . . Gob's rude . . . but I said gobSTOPPER – that's just a sweet . . .
Queen	It was the way you said it, Daphne. It was most hurtful to your mother.

[*A difficult truce. They sit down again. The* MC *meanwhile has returned with two bows and two quivers of arrows.* CYRIL *and the* BARON *put their quivers on their backs. The target is moved into position*]

MC	The Rules of the Archery Contest. You will fire off one arrow and one arrow only. The winner will be the one whose arrow is nearest the middle. Do you understand?
Cyril	Perfectly.
Baron	Sort of.
MC	Cyril, would you like to fire off first, please?
Cyril	Absolutely.
MC	In your own time, Cyril. Complete quiet please while Cyril pulls his string.

[CYRIL *fires his arrow. It goes in the inner. Note: See Appendix II*]

MC	Not quite in the bull. An inner.
Cyril	O really? Not quite in the bull, eh? O.
MC	Baron, would you like to fire off now please.
Baron	Yes I suppose so.

[*The* BARON *pulls his string back.* DAPHNE *sneezes. The arrow goes in* FAZ's *ear. Meanwhile* TWOO *is busy sticking another arrow into the target and saying:*]

Twoo	Ooo look! The Baron's scored a bull.
Faz	Phoorrrr! Ouch! Twoo!

Twoo	Right in it look!
Faz	[*Struggling to pull the arrow out*] Twoo! Can you get this arrow out of my ear please . . .
	[TWOO *and the* BARON *pull the arrow out. It takes some heaving, and the force sends* FAZ *flying into the Mechanical Scorer, which explodes and fizzes*]
Faz	Yahhhhhh!
Baron	I'm terribly sorry.
Faz	[*Doing his nut*] Sorry! You weedy clown!! You useless stringy bungler!!!
	[FAZ *chases the* BARON *out.* TWOO *follows on behind*]
MC	Your Majesties, yor Royal Highness, my Lords, Ladies and Gentlemen. Baron Wadd seems to have retired from the match, so I nominate as Winner of the Big Sporting Contest – natty comely Cyril the Fiddler.
Crowd	Boooooh!
MC	And a hand for the loser – repulsive Baron Wadd!
	[FAZ *chases the* BARON *across the stage,* TWOO *following*]
Crowd	Hoooorrraaayyyy!
MC	Do you want to say a few words your Majesty?
King	O yes. All right.
Daphne	Don't make an idiot of yourself, Dad.
Queen	Quiet, Daphne.
King	Ahem. Well I think we've all seen some very exciting Sport here today. As you all know the Winner, spruce, dapper Cyril the Fiddler, will shortly be marrying, Her Royal Highness Princess Daphne.
Daphne	But he wears red pants.
Queen	Quiet Daphne.
King	Well I'd just like to take this opportunity of inviting you all to the Royal Wedding. Thank you. Carry on. Keep it up Cyril.
	[*The* KING *and Queen start to go.* CYRIL *tries to take* DAPHNE*'s arm*]
Daphne	Ugh! Get your hairy muscly arm off me!

Cyril	But I've won you! I've won you!
Queen	He's won you Daphne. Don't be so silly.
Daphne	I want a bottle of beer. Have you got one?
Cyril	I wouldn' have got where I am today if I ever took alcohol, Daphne. [*A bit shocked,* CYRIL *is*]
	[TWOO *must have heard this because he races on and produces a bottle of beer from his pocket.* CYRIL *gapes.* TWOO *opens the bottle on* CYRIL*'s teeth. He puts a straw in it. He dashes off.* DAPHNE *blows him a kiss*]
Daphne	The sword that is blue is the sword that is true; The sword with the ball is no good at all.
Cyril	But Daphne I've won you!
	[DAPHNE *kicks* CYRIL *in the shins and runs off.* CYRIL *runs after her*]
Cyril	What have I done, Daphne? I thought we could be such chums!
	[*With difficulty*] I love you, Daphne . . . [*Boldly*] I love you!!
	[*As* DAPHNE *and* CYRIL *disappear,* FAZ, TWOO *and the* BARON *re-appear*]
Faz	Well that's that! You haven't got the Princess. And we haven't got our eight hundred thousand pounds!!
Baron	I know.
	[TWOO *has put the bucket down.* FAZ *sits in it*]
Faz	Just a minute . . .
Baron	What?
Twoo	Shhh I think he's got a plan coming on.
Faz	[*Like Custer*] We'll make a last-ditch stand! We'll disrupt the wedding!! We'll kidnap Cyril!!!!
Baron	Brilliant Faz, but how will you do it?
Faz	The Paraphernalia Case, Twoo?
Twoo	Are we going to do Paraphernalia, Faz?
Faz	Just give me the Paraphernalia Case, Twoo.
	[TWOO *gives it to him*]
Twoo	You've never seen us do our Paraphernalia have you?

Baron   No. I've heard of it of course.

Twoo   O it's fantastic, isn't it Faz?

Faz   Well it's pretty remarkable, yes!

              [*Suddenly the three laugh and fiendish about*]

Faz, Twoo & Baron
              [*Together*] To Buckingham Palace!

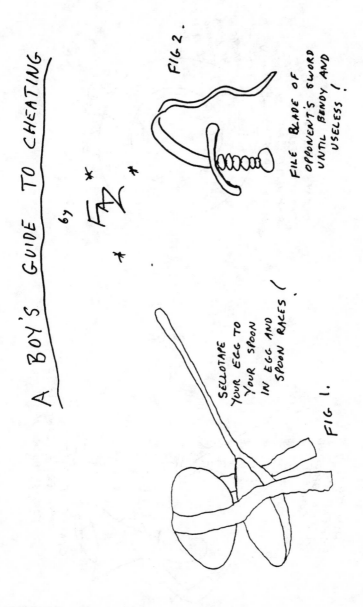

A BOY'S GUIDE TO CHEATING

by

FM **

FIG 2.

FILE BLADE OF
OPPONENT'S SWORD
UNTIL BENDY AND
USELESS!

SELLOTAPE
YOUR EGG TO
YOUR SPOON
IN EGG AND
SPOON RACES!

FIG. 1.

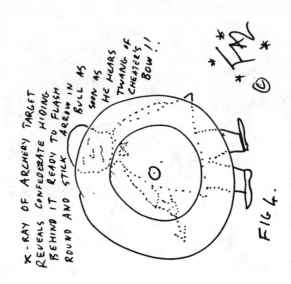

X - RAY OF ARCHERY TARGET REVEALS CONFEDERATE HIDING BEHIND IT READY TO FLASH ROUND AND STICK ARROW IN BULL AS SOON AS HE HEARS TWANG OF CHEATER'S BOW !!.

FIG 4.

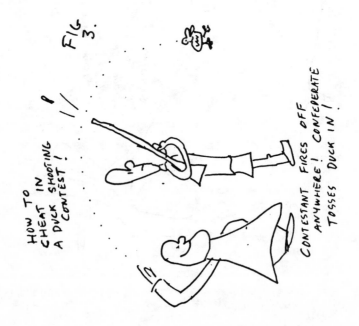

FIG 3.

HOW TO CHEAT IN A DUCK SHOOTING CONTEST !

CONTESTANT FIRES OFF ANYWHERE! CONFEDERATE TOSSES DUCK IN !.

Act 2

Scene the First and Only

[*The Main Hall of Buckingham Palace*]

[*The* BARON *comes in followed by* FAZ *and* TWOO. FAZ *and* TWOO *look about them for the moment overcome by the gold and gilt of the Palace, and the thick red carpet on the floor*]

Baron   The is the main hall of Buckingham Palace, Faz. The throne's just through there if you want it.

[*But Faz is lost in thought*]

Baron   What's the matter, Faz?

Twoo   [*With reverence*] I think he's thinking

Baron   O.

Faz   Let's have a sausage, Twoo. [TWOO *gives him one. Faz puts it in his mouth thoughtfully*] I think . . . there may be . . . a snag.

Twoo   Snag, Faz?

Faz   Snag yes.

Baron   Snag in the Paraphernalia plan you mean?

Faz   Precisely.

Baron   How do you mean Faz?

Faz   Well Twoo will bear me out here, but I've never known Paraphernalia to fail . . .

Twoo   No. Paraphernalia is fantastic.

Baron   Well – ?

Faz   But you know, I think there's a chance it won't work on Cyril the Fiddler.

Baron   Faz, why?

Twoo   Why, Faz?

Faz   Well, will it work on a Sports Champion? That's what I ask myself. I suppose it will if we use the really wild Paraphernalia. But 'twould be as well to be sure.

Twoo	Twould it Faz?
Faz	Twould Twoo, yes. [*Cuffs him*]
Baron	But why do you think Paraphernalia won't work on a Sports Champion? Why should a Sports Champion be any different from anyone else?
Faz	It's all the training they do. All the keep fit exercises. It gives them an incredible cool, clear-thinking mind. A Sports Champion might well see through Paraphernalia.
Baron	O Lord. So what're we going to do?
Twoo	Faz'll think of an answer.
Faz	Ahh!
Twoo	Here it comes.
Faz	Well. A Sports Champion would see through our Paraphernalia, but a DAZED Sports Champion would'nt.
Baron	A dazed Sports Champion. Dazed.
Faz	Precisely Baron. We've got to daze Cyril just before the wedding.
Twoo	Daze? What's that mean?
Faz	Bonk him on the head. Make him go umpy-doodly.
Baron	Fiendish Faz. But how?
	[TWOO *produces a large mallet.* FAZ *takes it and muses*]
Faz	I don't think this'd make any impression on him. He's a top notch sporto, 'n' he. Golden Gloves for Boxing he's got.
Baron	Yes.
Faz	See, you could bonk away at a Golden Glove Boxer's head for half an hour with one of these things and it wouldn't make any difference.
Baron	O.
Faz	No, it's going to take something pretty big to daze Cyril. How long have we got before the wedding. What's the time, Twoo?
	[TWOO *brings out his alarm clock on a chain and consults it*]
Twoo	Both the hands are pointing to that one at the top Faz.
Faz	Hmmmm. Twelve o'clock. Half an hour to go before the wedding. So we'll have to think up something quick.

[TWOO *can't resist making the alarm clock ring*]

Faz [*Biffs* TWOO] Stop it Twoo. We're trying to think here. Now what could we rig up?

Baron Rig up?

Twoo You mean a trap, Faz?

Faz Of course a trap, yes. The only query is, what trap? Twoo, have you got my book of traps on you. We might get an idea from that.

[TWOO *brings out an enormous book entitled:*

TRAPS for ALL by FAZ

The BARON *is most impressed and examines it closely*]

Baron *Traps for All* by Faz. You wrote it then?

Faz Yes.

Twoo Haven't you ever seen it before? It's a fantastic book, isn't it Faz?

Faz Well it's pretty amazing, yes. Anyway let's see if there's anything in it.

[FAZ *and the* BARON *get down on the floor on their fronts to have a look through it.* TWOO *sits beside them*]

Baron What about this 'Prune Baited Milkman Dangler'?

Faz No. Takes too long to set up. You need a couple of cranes.

[A box walks on. Only TWOO *sees it]*

Baron   O.

Twoo   *[Who thinks praps he'd better tell* FAZ *about the walking box]* Faz . . ?

Faz   Quiet Twoo. Shut up. *[To* BARON] This 'Sardine Baited Postman Trap' is a distinct possibility.

Baron   But Cyril's not a Postman.

Faz   *[If only he'd look up he'd see that the box is now doing a little dance, but he doesn't]* That don't matter. I only call it a Postman Trap because that's what it's normally used for, trapping Postmen. I mean you often need to trap a Postman . . .

Baron   Yes. Mmmm.

Faz   But trapping a Sporto, that doesn't often crop up.

Baron   No.

Twoo   *[Who has been watching the box all along]* Faz . . ?

Faz   Quiet Twoo, please.

Baron   This is a smashing book, Faz . . ?

Faz   You think it's all right do you?

Baron   I think it's so smashing.

Twoo   Faz . . ? A box has just walked on.

Faz   *[In a fury]* Quiet will you Twooooo!!!! *[In his rage he happens to have turned to page 804]* Ah! Here we are! This is it! 'The Messy Clothes Wag Trap'!!

Baron   The Messy Clothes Wag Trap?

Faz   Just the job isn't it. Cos he's a bit of a Wag, Cyril, a bit of a Toff. A natty dresser. Here! And he'll be in all his best clothes! His Wedding Clobber! His swanky togs! This is the trap boys, this is the feller! The Messy Clothes Wag Trap.

Baron   It's fiendish is it, Faz?

Faz   You ain't seen nothing fiendisher! *[Reminiscing with* TWOO] I say, The Messy Clothes Wag Trap, Twoo!! Eh??

Twoo   Yes! Actually I can't really remember it Faz. I do forget things fairly quickly.

Faz	Anyway, it's the answer Baron. [*He bumps into the box*] Ouch! Where did this box come from?
Twoo	It walked on Faz.
Faz	Walked on?
Twoo	While you were sun-bathing.
Faz	Walked on?
Twoo	Yes Faz.
Faz	Boxes don't walk. They don't walk around, boxes. They just sit on their bottoms and stay where they've been put. [*He clips* TWOO'*s Ear*]
Twoo	Well this one walks about. Doesn't it?
Audience	Twould seem so.
Faz	O no it doesn't.
Audience	O yes it does.
Faz	O no it doesn't.
Audience	O yes it does.
Twoo	It does Faz.
Faz	Quiet Twoo. [*Generally*] Quiet. And we weren't sun-bathing, we were scheming.
Twoo	O.
Baron	It's easy to rig up then is it, Faz, the Messy Clothes Wag Trap?
Faz	Yeah. Won't take a minute. Page 804, Baron. Read out the What You'll Need for this Trap List.
Baron	[*Having found page 804, he reads out*] One. Bubble Mixture. With Whatsname.
Faz	[*To* TWOO] Got your bubbles and whatsname?
	[TWOO *brings out his Bubble Mixture tube*]
Faz	Where's your whatsname?
Twoo	It's in the tube Faz.
Faz	Well check it. Make sure it is.
	[TWOO *unscrews the top of the tube and pulls out the whatsname.* FAZ *blows a test bubble through it*]

Faz	Yes. That's all right.
	[TWOO *blows a few bubbles through it*]
Faz	[*Giving him a little cuff on the head*] All right. All right. Put it away. Next.
Baron	Mountaineering Rope and Clip.
Faz	Mountaineering Rope and Clip.
Twoo	Yes. [*He shows them that he's got it all right*]
Faz	Good. Next.
Baron	Three. Pint of Oil approx.
Faz	Pint of Oil?
Twoo	I think so. [*He shows his oil can*] Yes.
Faz	Next.
Baron	Pulley Wheels, two.
Faz	Pulley Wheels, two.
Twoo	[*Showing his two pulley wheels*] Pulley Wheels two.
Faz	Good. Next.
Baron	Five. A Washing machine.
Faz	A Washing Mashine?
	[TWOO *looks through his pockets*]
Twoo	No Faz.
Faz	Won't be difficult to get hold of one. What else?
Baron	Six. A Ton Weight.
Twoo	No.
Faz	Right. All we've got to get is a Washing Machine and a Ton Weight and we're off.
Baron	Fantastic. You know Faz, I'd love to have a copy of this book.
Faz	Would you?
Baron	Yes.
Faz	Well you can have that one if you like Baron.
Baron	[*Moved*] O Faz. But what about you?

Faz	I've got lots more copies back at home. In fact I've got all the copies that were ever done. It didn't sell quite as well as I'd hoped.
Baron	O but it's a fantastic book Faz.
Twoo	It is fantastic isn't it. And it didn't sell any at all.
Baron	Thank you Faz. I shall always treasure this.
Faz	Shall I sign it for you?
Baron	Ooo yes please.
Faz	Pen.

[TWOO *gives* FAZ *a pen.* FAZ *signs the book*]

Twoo	Ought I to sign it as well Faz? Because I did think up a bit of one of them didn't I?
Faz	No. The Baron doesn't want you making puddly ink messes all over his nice new book, does he.
Twoo	No Faz.

[FAZ *signals to* TWOO *to get his camera out.* FAZ *and the* BARON *take up a pose, holding the book with one hand and leaning on the box with the other*]

Faz	It is with great pride, Baron Wadd, that I present you with my book *Traps for all* by Faz, which as you see I've signed.
Baron	Gosh thank you Faz.

[FAZ *and the* BARON *hold the position of giving and receiving the book, which is difficult owing to the great weight of the book*]

Faz	Cheese.
Baron	Cheese.

[*But the camera doesn't seem to be working*]

Faz	Cheese. Hurry up Twoo, this book's heavy.
Baron	Cheese.

[*The book is too heavy, and they totter to the floor*]

Twoo	It seems to be bunged up, Faz. I think it's got a bit of pocket dirt up the works.
Faz	Let's have a look.

[FAZ *inspects the camera. He pulls a bit of fluff out of it. The box walks a few feet to the right. No-one notices this*]

Faz	Try it now.
	[FAZ *and the* BARON *take up their positions in front of where the box was*]
Faz	[*Getting back into the mood*] . . . Pride Baron Wadd, that I present you with this my book, *Traps for All* by Faz, which as you see I've signed.
Baron	Gosh thank you Faz.
Faz & Baron	[*Together as they lean backwards on to the bit of air where once was a box, and fall over*] Cheese!
Camera	Flash! Thhhhppp! [*Snowstorm!!!*] Cuck-ooo!!!!
Twoo	Got it.
Faz	What do you mean you got it? That'll look super in the Album won't it. A picture of me romping and sprawling with the Baron. A snap of the Baron's stringy legs sticking up in the air.
Twoo	Yes Faz.
Faz	We'll have to take another one. Who moved this box anyway?
Twoo	I expect it walked Faz.
Faz	Boxes don't walk!!!!!
Twoo	O yes they do.
Faz	O no they don't.
Audience	[*Egged on by* TWOO] O yes they do.
Faz	O shut up! Shut up getting them going Twoo! Take another one. sitting on the box Baron.
	[BARON *and* FAZ *sit on the box*]
Faz	O no they don't.
Audience	O yes they do.
	[FAZ *gets off the box to yell at the audience. The* BARON *gets off too to back him up*]
Faz & Baron	[*Together*] O no they don't.
	[*The box walks away a few feet while they're yelling.* FAZ *and the* BARON *jump backwards to sit on where the box should have been and again fall over*]
Twoo	Watch the birdy.

Faz	O put it away Twoo. We can't waste time taking snaps. What is the time?

[TWOO *consults his alarm clock*]

Twoo	The little hand's pointing at the top one but the big one has moved round that much.
Faz	Mmmmm. Eight minutes past twelve. Come on Baron. You've footled away eight minutes. Twenty two minutes to the wedding. We must get the Messy Clothes Wag Trap rigged up right away.
Baron	Yes.
Faz	Twoo, you trot off and get a Washing Mashine; me and the Baron'll go and get a Ton Weight.
Twoo	Yes Faz.
Faz	What've you got to get?
Twoo	Errrm, er, a . . . .
Faz	Washing Machine.
Twoo	Washing Machine.
Faz	Correct. Right Baron, you come with me.

[FAZ *and the* BARON *go off to search Buchingham Palace for a Ton Weight*]

Twoo	Right . . . What've I got to get?
Audience	Washing Machine!!!!
Twoo	O yes. Where'm I going to get a washing mashine then?
Box	[*In a funny voice*] There's one just out through there.
Twoo	O thank you.

[TWOO *is about to go but the box keeps following him. He chases it away. But then it gets its courage back and starts following him again*]

Twoo	There's someone in it. Do you think I ought to open it and see who it is?
Audience	Yes. Open the box.

[TWOO *creeps up on the box but it moves away. He chases it. Eventually he corners it. He opens it. Up pops* PRINCESS DAPHNE]

Daphne	Hello.
Twoo	Hello.
	[*They have a little play and prod with each other*]
Twoo	Why are you in that box?
Daphne	I came to look for you. But I didn't want Brenda to know, so I hid in this box.
Twoo	Do you call your Mum Brenda?
Daphne	Yeah. Where's your nose?
Twoo	It's just here look.
Daphne	No, where's the red warty one you had at the Sports?
Twoo	At the Sports? O yes. I was in disguise then. You mean this.
	[TWOO *takes out his number forty-eight*]
Daphne	Put it on.
	[TWOO *puts it on*]
Daphne	That's much better.
	[*They have a little play and prod*]
Daphne	Listen, I'm in a fix.
Twoo	Can't you get out?
Daphne	No I can get out all right. [*And she does so. We can now see that she is wearing her wedding dress, which she has tucked into her knickers*] I don't want to marry this Cyril.
Twoo	Don't you?
Daphne	Big-headed sporty fiddler. No. Especially now it's out that he wears red pants.
Twoo	Well listen that's all right. Shall I tell you why?
Daphne	Why?
Twoo	Well you see me and Faz are going to do Paraphernalia at your wedding, right at the last minute, and we are going to kidnap Cyril. So you won't have to marry him at all. So that's all right.
Daphne	You're going to do Paraphernalia?
Twoo	Yes.
Daphne	What's that?

Twoo	O it's fantastic.
Daphne	What happens?
Twoo	Well – well you can't really describe. But . . . well it's fantastic.
Daphne	Will I like it?
Twoo	O yeah, you'll like it all right.
Daphne	Shall we do it now then?
Twoo	No we can't.
Daphne	Why not
Twoo	Well you can't really do it without Faz. You see he invented Paraphernalia, Faz, and you have to have him there for it otherwise it's just nothing.
Daphne	O. Well that's super. So I won't have to marry that awful Cyril.
Twoo	No. We're going to make sure you marry Baron Wadd all right.
Daphne	O good. What?
Twoo	Where?
Daphne	Who? Who did you say you were going to make sure that I marry?
Twoo	Baron Wadd.
Daphne	I don't want to marry Baron Wadd.
Twoo	O. Don't you?
Daphne	No.
Twoo	O. Who do you want to marry now then?
Daphne	Don't you know?
Twoo	No.
Daphne	Can't you guess?
Twoo	No.
Daphne	[*Goes all shy and silly, to the audience*] Tell him, will yer.
Audience	You, you half-wit.
Twoo	Me?
Audience	Yes.
Daphne	Yes. That's all right isn't it?

Twoo	Yes. I'd quite like that.
Daphne	Yes. I want to find out the secret of your pockets.
Twoo	[*Keeping out of her way*] Lots of people do.
Daphne	Have you got a – [*She tries to think up the most astonishing food combination ever*] – kipper and custard sandwich?
Twoo	Yes I think so. [*He ferrets in his pocket. Pulls out a Kipper and custard sandwich*] Here you are. I'm afraid it was made with margarine though.
Daphne	You're my man. Definitely. Is anything the matter, Twoo?
Twoo	Well look if we get married . . .
Daphne	Yes?
Twoo	We won't have any of that soppy kissing, or anything will we?
Daphne	Ughhh! No.
Twoo	No. That's all right then. Because I am a gangster you know. I'd better go and get this washing machine.
The Queen's Voice	[*Speaking from the next room*] Daphneeeee!
	[*She sounds very cross*]
Daphne	Crumbs. Mum!
The Queen's Voice	Any sign of her, Charlie?
The King's Voice	No. Any sign of her, Cyril?
Cyril's Voice	No.
Daphne	O Lor' They're all coming. And we haven't made a plan yet.
Twoo	No.
Daphne	Could you do me?
Twoo	Do you?
Daphne	Do my voice?
Twoo	[*Impersonating* DAPHNE] What like this you mean?
Daphne	That's super. You get in the box and disguise yourself as old rags.
	[TWOO *gets into the box.* DAPHNE *leaps into the audience. Enter* OLD KING COLE. OLD QUEEN COLE *and* CYRIL *looking for* DAPHNE]

Queen	Daphne! Where are you?
King	Come along Daphne! There's a good girl. Can't see her, Brenda.
Cyril	Come on Daffers. A jape's a jape, but this is going too far.
Queen	Daphne! come here instantly!
Cyril	O Daphne darling please. It's nearly wedding time.

[*They are standing in front of the box. The* QUEEN *on one side, the* KING *on the other and* CYRIL *in the middle. Unseen by any of them* TWOO *gives the* KING *a poke in the bottom with a broom-pole. The* KING *thinks* CYRIL *must have done it*]

King	What's the game, Cyril. [*He gives* CYRIL *a biff*]
Cyril	I say look here.

[TWOO *gives the* QUEEN *a poke in the bottom with his pole*]

Queen	[*Also assuming it must be* CYRIL] Do you mind? [*She slaps* CYRIL]
Daphne	[*Who is down in the audience*] What are you looking for Mum?
Queen	We're looking for Daphne, Daphne. [*Suddenly realising!!!*] Daphneee! There she is Charlie, come on. Come on Cyril.

[CYRIL *and the* QUEEN *go chasing after* DAPHNE, *while the* KING *stays on stage shouting encouragement. Suddenly he's knocked flat by the box. He gets up outraged*]

King	What's the game here?

[*The* KING *goes to investigate the box. The box charges him and knocks him over again*]

King	It's a revolution! It's a coup!

[*The* KING *draws his sword. But the box boxes clever. But the* KING *once took bull-fighting lessons from one of the top Spanish matadors. The* KING *fights the box as if it were a bull. Meanwhile* DAPHNE *has left the audience. She dashes across the stage. Not far behind her are the* QUEEN *and* CYRIL]

Queen	[*Seeing the* KING *fighting the box*] Charlie stop playing with that box! Come on! [*She clouts the* KING *and he follows her off after* DAPHNE]

[DAPHNE *comes back on. She seems to have given them the slip for the moment. She comes over to the box and taps on it*]

Daphne	It's all right, Twoo. It's me.
	[TWOO *pops up out of the box*]
Daphne	I've got an idea. Have you got any guns or anything?
Twoo	Yes I've got some guns and bombs. We usually use bombs in the Paraphernalia you see.
Daphne	Well that's it.
Twoo	What's it?
Daphne	Who's it?
Twoo	You're it. Had yer.
Daphne	Had yer back.
Twoo	Had yer.
Daphne	Had yer back.
Twoo	Had yer.
Daphne	Had yer back.
	[*This developes into a play and prod*]
Daphne	No listen. After you do this Paraphernalia at the wedding and this Faz has carted off Cyril, you bring out your guns, and we'll hold everyone up and make them let us get married. That's a super idea isn't it?
Twoo	Yes. That should work.
	[*Meanwhile the* QUEEN *comes on some way behind* DAPHNE. *She sees* DAPHNE *and beckons on the* KING. *The* KING *has got a huge shrimping net. He very slowly creeps forward with his shrimping net raised high in the air intending to catch* DAPHNE *in it*]
Daphne	[*Seeing consternation in the audience*] What's the matter?
Audience	[*Just making a confused noise*] Kibbyiyou! Kibbyiyou!
Daphne	What?
	[*The* KING *is now behind her with the net*]
Audience	[*Screaming*] Kingsbehindyouwivanet!!!!!
	[*But Too late. The* KING *catches her. He leads her off triumphantly. followed by the* QUEEN *and* CYRIL]
Queen	Come along Daphne and let's have no more of this silliness.

[*As the* KING *and Co go off,* FAZ *comes on*]

Faz   Twoooo! Get out of that box!!!

Twoo   O yes Faz. Sorry Faz.

Faz   Have you found a washing mashine yet?

Twoo   Washing mashine, Faz?

Faz   Washing Machine, yes. Have you found one?

Twoo   Nearly. I'm getting warmer.

Faz   Well hurry up. Me and the Baron have got a ton weight. We've just got to take the doors off to get it through.

[TWOO *gets out of the box and goes off in search of the washing machine.* FAZ *has gone to help the* BARON *with the Ton Weight*]

Faz   [*Off*] That's it Baron. Right a bit. Left a bit. Yes. No.

[FAZ *and the* BARON *come on struggling under an immense weight. Really huge it is. On it is written. 'ONE-TON'*]

Faz   [*Off*] Right hand down a bit. Left hand up a bit.

Baron   I'm dropping it! I'm dropping it!

Faz   Hang on Baron. All right. Down here.

[*They put one side down*]

Faz   Right let it go.

[*The* BARON *drops it on* FAZ'*s toe*]

Faz   Yaaaaaaaaaaaaaaaaaaah! [*He capers and dances with the pain. He takes off his plimsoll and sock. His big toe is a violent purple*] Phorrrrrrrr!

[TWOO *has come back in by now with news of a washing machine*]

Twoo   Hey Faz . . . Cor i'n't your toe a funny colour.

Faz   A most amusing hue, yes.

Baron   Rub some butter on it.

Faz   Butter?

Baron   Yes, butter is soothing for bruises.

Faz   Butter, Twoo, please.

[TWOO *produces a slice of bread and butter and gives it to* FAZ]

Faz	Haven't you got like a bar of butter?
Twoo	No Faz. I spread it on the bread.

[FAZ *wipes his toe with the bread and butter*]

Faz, Twoo & Baron
Errrrrrrgh!

[FAZ *makes the bread and butter into a sort of poultice, which with great difficulty he manages to keep on his toe when he walks*]

Twoo	I've found a washing machine. But it's a bit heavy for me.
Faz	All right. Hang on a minute. Right. Come on Baron let's get this washing machine.

[*The three go off and come back lugging a washing machine*]

Faz	That's it. Just here. Drop it here.

[*They drop it on* FAZ's *other foot*]

Faz	Yaaaaaaaah!

[*He takes off his other plimsoll and sock. His big toe on this foot has gone green!*]

Twoo	Oooo that one's green, Faz.
Faz	Pretty isn't it.
Twoo	Yes.

[TWOO *takes out another slice of bread and butter and hands it to* FAZ. FAZ *throws it at* TWOO. *It sticks onto the back of* TWOO's *coat*]

Faz	Time.

[TWOO *takes out his alarm clock*]

Twoo	The little one's sort of still at the top one but the big one has moved on that much.
Faz	Hmmmmm. Twelve twenty. Ten minutes to the wedding, We've got to set this trap up quick if we're gonna daze Cyril in time. Right, Twoo. Got your rope?
Twoo	Yeah.
Faz	Yer two pulley wheels?
Twoo	Yeah.
Faz	Right. Like lightning. Round the back. Under the wotsit. Up the doings. And into the rafters. When you get up there dangle your rope down to us.

Twoo	Get up in the rope and dangle me rafters.
Faz	Up in the rafters, dangle your rope!
Twoo	O yes.
	[*A clout sends* TWOO *on his way*]
Faz	Right Baron. Let's get to work. We've got to gut the washing mashine.
Baron	Gut it?
Faz	Get all the workings and gubbins out.
Baron	Why?
Faz	Twoo's got to get in it, hasn't he.
Baron	O.
	[FAZ *opens the top of the washing machine and he and the* BARON *yank all the workings out of it. While* FAZ *has got the whole top half of his body buried in the washer, wrestling with a stubborn item of the workings, the* BARON *finds a bit that interests him*]
Baron	This is the switch isn't it Faz? This is what switches it on.
Faz	[*Still in the washer*] Hmmmm?
	[*The* BARON *switches the switch. There is a minor explosion in the washer.* FAZ *emerges with a black face*]
Faz	[*Calmly*] That's right Baron. That's what switches it on. [*Clouts him*]
	[TWOO's *rope starts to descend from the ceiling. It's the end of the rope with the clip on*]
Faz	Good man Twoo. More. More. Enough. Hold it.
Baron	This is fiendish.
Faz	Got your pulleys Twoo? Good. Screw them into the rafters. And pass your end of the rope over them. Got that? And then dangle your end down. [FAZ *clips the rope onto the ring on the top of the Ton Weight*] I'll hang on to that lot. [*Referring to the workings*] It could come in handy as spare Paraphernalia.
Baron	O Yes. What now?
Faz	We've got to wait for the other end of the rope. Hurry up Twoo.

Reprinted from page 804 of 'Traps for All' by FAZ

FAZ's Remarkable Messy Clothes Wag Trap

What You'll Need For This Trap
1. Bubble Mixture. With Whatsname
2. String
3. Pint of Oil Approx.
4. Pulley Wheels, two
5. Washing Machine
6. Ton Weight
and, of course, shears.

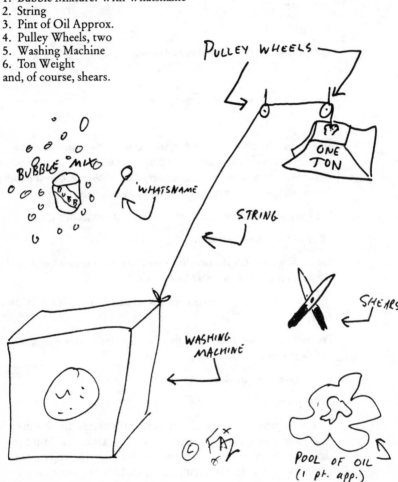

[*The other end of the rope starts to come down*]

Faz   That's it. Let it go. All the way. That's it. Great. Now belt back down here again, Twoo. Where are you? Ah there you are. Belt back down here, mate, cos we're gonna need you to help on the hoisting. Wish I had a sausage.

Baron   I don't quite see how it works.

Faz   You'll see. This is almost it. It's really just a question of hoisting now. You haven't got such a thing as a sausage on you have you?

Baron   No. [*He thinks of a funny*] Not a sausage!

Faz   O shut up.

[TWOO *returns*]

Faz   Good work Twoo. Come here. That's it. Right. Hoist.

Baron   Me as well?

Faz   O yes. It'll take the combined strength of all of us to get that up. Ready?

[*The* BARON *joins* FAZ *and* TWOO *on the rope*]

Baron & Twoo   [*Together*] Yeah.

Faz   Heave![*They strain their hardest on the rope but the Ton Weight doesn't move*] And again! Heave! [*Still they can't shift the Ton Weight.* FAZ *makes an appeal for help to the audience*] Listen! Give us a bit of encouragement, can't you, or we're never going to shift the thing. Right! With me – Heave!!!

Audience   Heave!!!!

[*The Ton Weight starts to go up*]

Faz   And again!

Audience   Heave!!!

[*The Ton Weight goes up a bit more*]

Baron   I'm trying my weedy best.

Faz   We're proud of you Baron. And again!

Audience   Heave!!!

[*The Ton Weight is now about eight feet off the ground. But the effort has taken its toll on the* BARON]

Baron	Hey Faz, my muscles are going all goobly!
Faz	Hang on Baron, hang on! If this weight drops now it could be curtains for us all!!!
	[FAZ *and* TWOO *hang on for grim death. The* BARON *has had to let go*]
Baron	I can't help it Faz. It happens when I get over-excited. Oooo me legs are getting the goobles now!
	[*The* BARON*'s legs go goobly under him and he falls down immediately under the Ton Weight*]
Faz	Baron!!! Get out from under that weight!!!
Baron	What?
Faz	You're under the weight! Get out of the way!!
Twoo	I think my arms are going to break off, Faz!
Faz	Hang on Twoo, hang on!! Baron!!
Baron	What? Sorry Faz? I'm not hearing properly. I get fuzz in the head when I'm goobly.
Faz	[*To audience*] Tell him will yer?!
Audience	Get out from under the weight, Baron!!
Baron	What?
Audience	The weight! The weight!!
	[BARON *looks up where people seem to be pointing. Suddenly realises he's looking up at the underside of the Ton Weight. He panics. But he can't move!*]
Baron	It's no good Faz! I can't move!! My muscles just don't respond!!!! I'm totally goobly!!!
Faz	What a time to go totally goobly!
Twoo	Faz! My arms!!
Faz	Hold on Twoo or it's bye bye Baron.
Baron	There's only one thing to do when I get like this. I have to sit very still and quiet and count up to thirty.
Faz	Thirty!
Baron	Yes it's the only thing to do when I get like this.
	[*The* BARON *sits in a meditative position counting.* FAZ *and* TWOO *are swinging about on the end of the rope in their desperation to hang on. The* BARON *sits for what seems hours. Then he opens his eyes*]

Faz	You all right now?
Baron	What comes after eight?
Twoo	Six.
Faz	Shut up Twoo!! Nine! Nine!
Baron	O yes. Then what? I know what it is but I can't think of the name of it.
Faz	Ten. [*To audience*] Count for him if you don't want him squashed!
Audience	10 – 11 – 12 – 13 – 14 – 15 – 16 – 17 – 18 – 19 – 20 – 21 –
Faz	Faster! Faster!
Audience	22–23–24–25–26–27–28–29–30.
Baron	Thirty! I'm all right. All the gooblies gone.
	[*The* BARON *jumps up and joins them on the rope.* FAZ *and* TWOO *let go in relief, the Weight comes down and the* BARON *goes up to the ceiling*]
Baron	Heeellllpppppppp!
	[FAZ *and* TWOO *pull the rope and the* BARON *comes down and the Weight goes up again.* FAZ *ties the rope to a bit of electrical flex on the washing machine. So the Weight is now gently swinging menacingly aloft*]
Faz	[*Not without pride*] Well that's it.
Baron	I'm sorry about that, Faz. Clout me if you want to.
Faz	No forget it. It's not your fault if you're weedy and get the goobles.
Baron	Thank you Faz.
Faz	Let's have a sausage, Twoo.
	[TWOO *gives* FAZ *a sausage*]
Baron	[*Who has noticed that* TWOO *never has a sausage*] You don't sausage then?
Twoo	About one a day. That's all. I used to sausage pretty heavily but I've managed to cut it right down now.
Faz	Come on. We haven't got time to footle away discussing Twoo's sausage habits. What is the time?

Twoo	[*Alarm clock out*] The little hand has moved on a bit from the top one and the biggy is this much away from the bottom.
Faz	Twelve-twenty-five! Five minutes to go before the wedding! There's every cause for panic! We've got about two minutes to daze Cyril.
Twoo	And make him umpy-doodly.
Faz	Twoo! Got your bubbles and shears!?
Twoo	Yes.
Faz	Right, get in the washing machine. Baron you keep a look out down there.
	[TWOO *gets inside the washing machine*]
Twoo	Shall I start blowing bubbles, Faz?
Faz	Yeah you might as well. Give us the oil.
	[TWOO *gives* FAZ *the can of oil. Then there are voices from the next room*]
The Queen's Voice	I'll just put your shirt in the washer, Charlie.
The King's Voice	Right-O Brenda. But hurry up. It's the wedding in four and a half minutes.
Baron	The Queen's just out there Faz!
Faz	Shhhh.
The Queen's Voice	Charlie! Someone's moved the washer!
Baron	Faz! She's coming this way!
Faz	Scarper! [BARON *and* FAZ *start to hare off into hiding*]
Twoo	What about me?
Faz	Get down! If she sees you, say you're fixing it!
Twoo	Fixing it.
Faz	If things get panicky, make frightening faces and silly noises. That should scare her off.
Twoo	Frightening faces and silly noises.
Faz	[*Seeing the* QUEEN *coming*] Get down!!

[*The* BARON *and* FAZ *have hidden themselves just in time.* TWOO *is crouching down in the washing machine. He opens the clothes porthole a little way and blows bubbles out of it. The* QUEEN *comes in. She is carrying a dirty shirt*]

Queen   Ah. Here it is.

[*She opens the clothes porthole and sticks the shirt in*]

Twoo   Do you want bleach?

Queen   No thank you.

[*The* QUEEN *shuts the clothes porthole and walks away. Suddenly she wonders who asked her about the bleach. She goes back to the washer and opens it again*]

Queen   What're you doing in my washing machine?

Twoo   I'm fixing it.

Queen   Fixing it?

Twoo   So that the rain won't get in.

Queen   Are you a half-wit?

Twoo   Yes.

[*The* QUEEN *almost trips over one of* FAZ's *plimsolls*]

Queen   Whose are these?

Twoo   Err, they're my mother's.

Queen   [*Noticing the washer workings and* FAZ's *toe bread and butter*] Whose is all this junk and old bread and butter?

Twoo   That's my mother's too.

Queen   Your mother's?

Twoo   It fell out of her knickers.

Queen   Get out of there! Get out of my washing machine you rude little man.

[TWOO *makes frightening faces and silly noises. The* QUEEN *panics and runs off.* FAZ *and the* BARON *return*]

Faz   Well done Twoo. Quick thinking about your mother. [*To audience*] not bad for a half-wit, was it?

Audience   Nooo! Pretty good!

Faz   Give him a cheer then.

Audience   Hoooooorraayyyy!

Twoo   Thank you Faz. [*To* AUDIENCE] Thank you. [*He gives a modest little bow*]

Baron   Can you explain to me quickly how this trap works, Faz?

Faz   Well it'll have to be quick. The Messy Clothes Wag Trap. The Wag, in this case Cyril, comes in here. I shall have put some oil down here. He slips over in the oil in his nice clothes. 'Errgh!' he says. 'My clothes are all messy. What shall I do?' Then he sees these bubbles what Twoo is blowing. The bubbles lead him to the washing machine. He takes off his clothes. He's about to pop them in through the clothes porthole, when Twoo pops up. Cyril boggles. He's now right under the Ton Weight. [FAZ *is standing right under the Ton Weight in order that the* BARON *can get the full picture*] Quick as a flash Twoo's out with his shears and snips the flex holding up the Ton Weight. [TWOO *goes to snip it*] Not now Twooooo!!!! [TWOO *realises just in time*] And so the Ton Weight comes thundering down on Cyril's head, thus dazing him.

Twoo   Making him umpy-doodly.

Baron   O fantastic Faz. O this is fiendish.

Faz   [*A big moment*] I shall put the oil down. [*He pours the can. There's nothing in it*] It's empty Twoo!! There's none in it!!!

Twoo   Isn't there?

Faz   O woe! Everthing rigged up and no oil! [*Despair*]

Twoo   [*Referring to the audience*] Couldn't they do something to help?

Faz   What the gawpers? Use the gawpers again you mean?

Twoo   Yes.

Baron   Would you be prepared to help?

Audience   Yes, yes, yes.

Baron   Yeah, they'll all help, Faz. What's the matter?

Faz   I always hate using amateurs in a trap. [*Aggressively to audience*] You reckon you're up to it do you?

Audience   Yeesss!!!

Faz	Well listen hard. We've got to work fast or we're sunk. When Cyril comes in here, all you lot on this side 'Hoy! Cyril!!!' Right? And when he turns round make frightening faces and silly noises at him. Got that? Now when Cyril hears those silly noises and sees those frightening faces he'll panic. He'll run over this way. Well, when he gets to here, I want everyone to blow at once, blow him over, you've got to blow him over, if you all blow at the same time, it'll be like a hurricane, see if you can blow me over. No, more. Put twice the puff into it. Really big, outrageous puffs, come on!!!!! [*The audience manage to blow* FAZ *over*] That's it! That's great! Now Cyril's clothes will now be a bit messy, but not nearly messy enough as there's no oil, so I want you all to shout 'Hoy Cyril, your clothes is all messy! Stick 'em in the washer!' Right, let's have a run through. I'll be Cyril. I don't know anything's going to happen.
	[FAZ *walks on as if he's* CYRIL]
Audience	Hoy! Cyril!
	[FAZ *turns round. The audience make frightening faces and silly noises at him.* FAZ *pretends to panic and runs away to the middle of the stage*]
Faz	This is where you blow! Come on blow!! [*They blow him over*] That's it!
	[FAZ *conducts the audience as they shout*]
Audience	Hoy Cyril, your clothes is all messy! Stick 'em in the washer!
Faz	Not bad. [*Talking to the audience in sections*] Do you lot know what to do?
First Lot	Yesss!
Faz	Do you lot know what to do??
Second Lot	Yeessss!!
Faz	Do you lot know what to do????
Third Lot	Yeeeesssss!!!!!
Baron	Faz! Here comes Cyril now!
Faz	To your places! Good luck men!
	[FAZ *and the* BARON *hide out of the way.* CYRIL *comes on in his smart wedding clothes*]

Audience	Hoy Cyril!
	[CYRIL *turns round. They make frightening faces and silly noises at him. He panics and runs to the middle of the stage. The audience blows him over*]
Audience	Hoy Cyril, your clothes is all messy! Stick 'em in the washer!!
Cyril	[*Genuinely appreciative*] O thank you.
	[CYRIL *takes off his messy clothes. We see he still wears those awful red pants. He goes to the washing machine. He bends down to open the clothes porthole . . .* TWOO *pops up, shears in hand . . .* CYRIL *boggles . . . He's now right under the Ton Weight . . .* TWOO *cuts the flex with his shears . . . and the Ton Weight comes thundering down on* CYRIL's *head. A great moment of Theatre*]
Faz	[*Triumphantly leaping out from cover*] It's worked!!! Right! Now to see if he's dazed!! Twoo get the other end! Lift up!
	[FAZ *and* TWOO *lift up the Ton Weight to let* CYRIL *out from under it.* CYRIL *staggers out. The weight has sent* CYRIL *into the land of the umpy-doodle. He walks like a silly chicken and talks like a parrot*]
Cyril	Adoy a doy a doy a rumpa do!
Baron	[*Leaping with delight*] It's worked!
Faz	[*Doing ecstatic cartwheels*] He's dazed!!
Twoo	Umpy-doodly!!! [*He does a joyful splits –*] Ouch! [*– except for the last bit*]
Faz	[*To audience*] Paraphernalia'll work on him now! No doubts about it!
	[CYRIL *is doing his silly chicken strut.* TWOO *follows him, trying to copy it*]
Cyril	Squawk! Squawk! Squawk! Hoy doy poingy doing! Roingy doingy doo! A doo!
Twoo	[*Giving him a hug*] I like him now he's umpy-doodly, Faz.
Faz	Put him down Twoo. What's the time?
Twoo	The little hand is half way between the top one and the one after the top one and the biggy is pointing at the bottom one.
Faz	Twelve thirty! Zero hour!! The Wedding's due to begin now!!!
Baron	I think I hear the Royal Party coming!

Faz	Paraphernalia Case, Twoo!
	[TWOO *fetches the Paraphernalia Case*]
Faz	[*Pulling out electrical flex from case, yards and yards of it, with a plug on the end. To* BARON] Where are your main circuits?
Baron	Where are my what?
Faz	Plug this in to the Main Wiring System!
	[*The* BARON *chases off with the plug end of the flex. The reel is still in the case and unwinds from there as he goes*]
Faz	Disguises, Twoo. We'll disguise ourselves as Foreign Wedding Guests! Foreign noses! [TWOO *brings out the foreign noses. They put them on*] And Fezzes.
Twoo	You want a Fez, Faz?
Faz	Yez. [TWOO *supplies fezzes*] And talk in Foreign.
Twoo	Talk in Foreign?
Faz	You know – Gobble Language!
Twoo	O yes, gooble gooble ob job twiddly?
Faz	Fath fath twinkle grobblers.
Cyril	Grobbly grobbly hoompy doo. [*Chicken strutting*] Squawk! Squawk!
Faz & Twoo	[*Together*] Squawk! Squawk! [*In their hysteria they take up* CYRIL'S *chicken strut*]
Baron	Here they come now!
Faz	All plugged in?
Baron	Yes.
	[*Enter the* VICAR, *who looks remarkably like the* MC *with a dog collar on*]
Vicar	My Lords, Ladies and Gentlemen, please be upstanding for His Majesty Old King Cole.
	[*Everybody including the audience, stands. Enter* OLD KING COLE, *splendidly dressed except that he hasn't got a shirt on. He is in his vest. Also* OLD QUEEN COLE, *very smart, and* DAPHNE *hating every thread of her wedding gown*]
King	Please sit down everybody.

[*Everybody sits down*]

King   Where's Cyril. Ah there he is. I say Cyril, I think you might have worn trousers for your wedding.

Cyril   [*Happily chicken strutting*] Squawk! Squawk!

King   Yes. Well we wont say any more about it as I had to come in my vest. Apparently there was a fiend in the washer.

Queen   Charlie, who brought our Ton Weight in here. O this is too much.

[TWOO *furtively pulls his false nose out so that* DAPHNE *can see that its him under it*]

Twoo   I've got the guns.

King   Right. Let's get the Wedding going shall we?

Vicar   Yes your Majesty. We are gathered here today . . .

King   [*Noticing* FAZ *and* TWOO *ferreting about in the Paraphernalia Case*] Just a minute. Baron!

Baron   Yes your Majesty?

King   Who on earth are those two extraordinary people?

Baron   They're Foreign Wedding Guests your Majesty.

King   O really! Foreign Wedding Guests! How do you do!

Faz   [*Hiding the Paraphernalia Case behind his back*] Glob glob goolie up your jumbole.

King   Is there? I mean, pardon?

Twoo   Hink widdle pooly pot.

King   Er yes. What are they saying, Baron?

Baron   Well I don't really know your Majesty. They don't speak English. Only Foreign. You know – Gobble Language.

King   O. Well hello!

Queen   Hello!

Faz   Goolie goolie!

Twoo   Up yer jumble!

King   Thank you. I hope yours does too. Right.

Vicar	We are gathered here today to witness the Marriage of Her Royal Highness Princess Daphne and that renowned figure of the Sporting and Musical World, Cyril the Fiddler. Will the Happy Couple step forward, please.

[DAPHNE *and* CYRIL *step forward*]

Vicar	Cyril the Fiddler, do you take Her Royal Highness Princess Daphne to be your lawful wedded Wife?
Cyril	I do I do I doodly doodly doo! Squawk!! Thhhhpppp!!!
Vicar	Er yes. Good.
Cyril	[*Turning round to the assembly. In a very coy, silly voice, blushing*] I feel very happy! Squawk!
Queen	Charlie, am I really the Queen or is this the Funny Farm?
Vicar	Your Royal Highness Princess Daphne do you take Cyril the Fiddler to be your lawful wedded Husband?
Daphne	[*Looking to* TWOO *to save her*] Er – I – d –

Faz, Twoo & Baron

[*Together, screaming*] PPPppppaaaaarrrapphheeerrrrnnnnnnaa-aaaaalllllliiaaaaaaaaaaaaaaaaaaaaahhhhhhhhhhhh!!!!!!!!!!!!!!!!! !!

[FAZ *plonks down the Paraphernalia Case right in front of the* VICAR. *Quick as lightning* FAZ *whips open the lid and takes out a dynamite detonation plunger and hands it to* TWOO *who races clear with it.* TWOO *presses down the dynamite detonation plunger. The lights go out and there is a wild flash under the* VICAR, *followed by a deafening boom! The lights then flash on and off with dazzling rapidity. Inside the Case is the most fantastic collection of gear imaginable. Sticks of celery, bicycle handlebars, fog horns, bells, rude noise cushions, jars out of which snakes leap when you undo the lids, confetti, monster hands, goggles, mop heads which one can use as wigs, balloons, balls on elastics, bugles, etc. etc.*]

[FAZ *and* TWOO *bring out this stuff bit by bit and caper about with it in the most wild and frantic manner imaginable. The* BARON *joins in. The idea is that you create a catching atmosphere of madness. First the victims will wonder what on earth is going on, but it is so catching that in the end they can't resist joining in. When they're really gone on it, the Paraphernalia perpetrators stop, leaving only the victims Paraphernaling. Then, in the midst of the havoc, they can get on with the Dirty Deed, in this case the kidnapping of* CYRIL]

| | [*And that is how it goes. When everyone has succumbed to the spell of Paraphernalia,* FAZ, TWOO *and the* BARON *bundle* CYRIL *into a sack and cart him off. They return. Then* TWOO *brings out a tommy gun and a blunderbuss. The lights return to normal*] |

Twoo   Daphne! [TWOO *tosses* DAPHNE *the tommy gun*]

Daphne   All right keep still everybody and no-one'll get hurt!

Twoo   Put your hands up.

Faz   Twoo! What on earth – ?

Daphne   And you, Baron.

Queen   What's this new silliness, Daphne?

Daphne   This is who I'm going to marry.

              [TWOO *removes his foreign nose and fez thus revealing his true identity*]

Queen   Charlie! It's that wretched little man who was in my washer!

Daphne   Come on Rev! Get marrying us then!

King   Just one moment young lady!

Daphne   [*Pointing gun at him*] Get back Dad!

              [*The* KING *stands his ground. Eventually* DAPHNE *points her gun away from him*]

Daphne   O Dad!

King   This is Great Britain. Not the Land of the Waggalooboo. However right you young people think you are, you mustn't get the idea that the only way to get things done is at gun point! This is Buckingham Palace, not Dodge City. We have a proper way of doing things here. It must be put to the Nation.

Vicar   You mean you want to take a vote on it your Majesty?

              [*The* KING *nods. The* VICAR *whips off his dog collar and black vicar dicky, revealing his* MC's *bow*]

MC   [*To audience*] Citizens of Great Britain! If it is your considered wish that Her Royal Highness Princess Daphne should not, I repeat NOT, marry the commoner Twoo, would you please raise your right hands now. This is if you think they should NOT get married.

              [*One or two foolish members of the audience raise their hands*]

| MC | If on the other hand it is your considered wish that Her Royal Highness Princess Daphne and the commoner Twoo SHOULD get married, please raise your right hands now! |

[All that can be seen are hands and hands and more hands!]

| MC | Your Majesty, by an overwhelming majority, the Country wants the marriage to take place!!! |

| Audience | Hooooraayyyyy!!!!! |

| King | *[To audience]* You're sure, are you? |

| Audience | Yeesssss! |

| King | Very well. Twoo come here. [TWOO *goes to the* KING] Take off your coat. [TWOO *takes off his coat. The* KING *draws his sword*] Kneel [TWOO *kneels*] From henceforward you shall be known as Duke Twoo [*He dubs him on the shoulders with his sword*] Rise Duke Twoo. [TWOO *gets up*] Let the Wedding continue. |

| MC | We are gathered here today . . . |

| Daphne | You can cut all that twaddle, Rev – I do. *[To* TWOO*]* How about you? |

| Twoo | Yeah, I do too. |

| MC | Well, I pronounce you man and wife, I suppose. Have you got a ring? |

*[*TWOO *produces a whole card of rings, like you see in a jeweller's window, out of his hip pocket.* DAPHNE *selects one]*

| Daphne | This one'll do. Right folks, let's go and leap on the Wedding grub! |

| MC | *[To audience]* Three cheers for the Red, White and Blue! Hip pip – |

| Audience | Hooray! |

| MC | Hip pip – |

| Audience | Hooooorrraaaayy!! |

[They all go off except for FAZ *and the* BARON. TWOO *has left his coat behind]*

| Faz | Well there you go Baron. [*He takes off his fez and nose and slings them into the Paraphernalia Case*] |

| Baron | Yes, Faz. Hasn't turned out quite as we hoped. |

Faz	Of course I'm very happy for Twoo. [*He doesn't look happy however. In fact he looks as if he might weep in a minute*] I mean he'll be King one day won't he. And I'm very happy for him. I can't think of anything nicer. [*He bursts into tears*] Baron?
Baron	Yes, Faz?
Faz	Do you think when he's King he'll ever think of me?
Baron	O I'm sure he will, Faz.
Faz	[*Bravely conquering his tears now*] Wish I had a sausage.
	[*The* BARON *suddenly notices that he's standing on* TWOO's *overcoat. He fishes out the sausage case and gives* FAZ *a sausage*]
Baron	Here you are, Faz.
Faz	O. Ta.
	[*The* BARON, *unseen by* FAZ *puts* TWOO's *coat on. He rather fancies himself in it*]
Baron	Faz . . .
Faz	Yes?
Baron	I was thinking now that you haven't got a feeble-minded assistant, would a weedy one do?
	[FAZ *turns round and sees the* BARON *in* TWOO's *coat. He walks round the* BARON, *inspecting him and musing*]
Faz	Hmmmmmmmm.
Baron	Go on, FAZ. Let us.
Faz	[*To audience*] What do you think, People of Great Britain? Shall I take him on?
Audience	Yeessssss!!
Faz	Yeah, all right, come on Baron! There' plenty more traps to be designed, schemes to scheme . . .
Baron	Plots to plot!
Faz & Baron	[*Together*] Dirty Deeds to Do!!!
Faz	Paraphernalia Case, Baron.
	[BARON *picks up the Case*]
Faz	A pleasure to have you in the Organisation, Baron.
Faz & Baron	Ta-ta Kids!!

Audience	Bye!!!!

[*And out they go.* MC *leaps on*]

MC	And that's really the end of our story. So it's Goodnight from Old King Cole and Old Queen Cole.

[OLD KING COLE *and* OLD QUEEN COLE *come on.* THE QUEEN *is carrying a money bag*]

King	[*To audience*] To celebrate the marriage of our daughter, I hereby decree that every poor person in the land shall have a Royal Penny.

Queen	Will the needy please raise their hands?

[*The* KING *and* QUEEN *throw pennies to needy*]

MC	It's Goodnight from Cyril!

[CYRIL *leaps on in his sporting gear. He is carrying a tennis racket. Cotton-wool snowballs are thrown at him from the side of the stage and he swipes them into the audience with his racket*]

MC	And Goodnight from Princess Daphne and Duke Twoo!

[TWOO *and* DAPHNE *come on*]

Daphne	[*To* TWOO] Toffees.

[TWOO *supplies her with a bag of toffees. She takes one herself and throws the rest out to the audience*]

MC	And finally Goodnight from the Amazing Faz and his Weedy Wonder Boy Baron Wadd!!

[*There is a flash and a boom and* FAZ *and the* BARON *appear.* FAZ *clicks his fingers.* BARON *brings out the sausage case.* FAZ *takes one and slings another couple out to the audience*]

All	Goodnight! God Bless!! Ta-ta!!! Cheerio!!!

[*The End*]

Appendix I

[*On open stage it might be felt desirable to add this scene onto the end of of Act One Scene One, to facilitate changing the setting from* FAZ*'s Office to Wembley Stadium*]

Baron   There is just one thing . . .

Faz   What?

Baron   Who's going to pay for the bus fares?

Faz   You are.

Baron   Ah yes. You see the thing is I am just a bit short at the moment Till I marry Daphne.

Faz   How much have you got?

Baron   Nothing.

Faz   What've we got, Twoo? Let's have a look in the tin.

[TWOO *passes* FAZ *their money box*]

Faz   One and a half p and eight buttons. Well that's not going to get us to Wembley is it?

Rag and Bone Men
[*Outside*] Rag and Bones! Rag and Bones!

Faz   Just a minute, once you've married Daphne we're all going to be loaded, aren't we? We won't need this dump of an office any more.

Baron   No. You can come and live in the Palace if you like and be my wicked henchmen.

Faz   O yeah. That'd be great. [*To* RAG AND BONE MEN] Oyyyy!

[TWOO *whistles.* RAG AND BONE MEN *come in*]

Faz   How much 'll you give me for my delightful fixtures, fittings and furnishings?

Bone Man   Fourpence.

Faz   Fourpence! Fifty p at least! Come now gentlemen!

Bone Man   You must be joking.

[FAZ *picks up one of the chairs*]

Faz	This is good gear, mate. Look at this magnificent, mahogany, fourteenth century, Jacobean – [*The chair he's holding falls to bits*] – firewood! And this hat-stand is almost useful.
Bone Man	Bob the lot
Faz	O all right.
	[RAG AND BONE MEN *cart everything off during following short scene*]
Faz	It'll pay for <u>our</u> fares anyway, Baron.
Baron	What about your feeble-minded friend?
Faz	Who? Twoo? He can trot along behind the bus. You can trot along behind the bus, Twoo.
Twoo	I've got to trot along behind the bus, Faz?
Faz	You don't expect the Baron to trot along behind it do you? With his stringy legs?
Twoo	No.
Faz	Well then. [*Clouting* TWOO] Right!

Faz, Twoo & Baron
[*Together*] To Wembley Stadium!

Appendix II

The Archery Contest

[The Arrow which CYRIL *takes out of his quiver for the Archery Contest DOES NOT EXIST. It is MIMED.* CYRIL *just pulls back his string and lets fly, and the* MC, *with expert timing either sticks an arrow in the Inner or, if a trick target is being used (see diagram), releases the catch. The* BARON's *shot is worked in more or less the same way. Except that in this case* FAZ *has a hidden arrow which he holds to his ear at the appropriate moment]*

Idea for a Trick Target

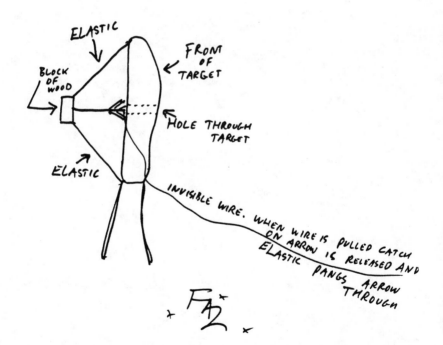

OBERON BOOKS LIMITED

32 Russell Road, Enfield, Middlesex EN1 4TY England
Tel: 01-367 9603   Fax: 01-363 2298

PUBLISHED TITLES

Apart from George	Nick Ward ISBN 1 870259 15 7
The Cabinet Minister	Pinero ISBN 1 870259 08 4
Court in the Act!	Marcel Hennequin and Pierre Veber, translated by Robert Cogo-Fawcett and Braham Murray ISBN 1 870259 04 1
Don Carlos *	Schiller, translated by James Maxwell ISBN 1 870259 06 8
Faust	Goethe, translated by Robert David MacDonald ISBN 1 870259 11 4
Joan of Arc/Mary Stuart	Schiller, translated by Robert David MacDonald ISBN 1 870259 07 6
Mean Tears/In the Blue	Peter Gill (two plays) ISBN 1 870259 05 X
No Orchids for Miss Blandish	Robert David MacDonald (from the novel by James Hadley Chase) ISBN 1 870259 13 0
Northern Star/Heavenly Bodies/Pentecost	Stewart Parker (three plays) ISBN 1 870259 17 3
Oedipus the King/ Oedipus at Colonus	Sophocles, translated by Christopher Stace ISBN 1 870259 03 3
The Pied Piper	Adrian Mitchell ISBN 1 870259 09 2
School for Wives §	Molière, translated by Robert David MacDonald ISBN 1 870259 02 5
The Strangeness of of Others	Nick Ward ISBN 1 870259 14 9
Woundings •	Jeff Noon ISBN 1 870259 00 9

TITLES TO BE PUBLISHED

Absolute Hell	Rodney Ackland ISBN 1 870259 19 X
Susan's Breasts/Naked Robots/The Paranormalist	Jonathan Gems (three plays) ISBN 1 870259 10 6 (for publication early 1990)
Enrico Four	Luigi Pirandello, translated by Robert David MacDonald (for publication early 1990)

§ Out of print, but to be published with another title in 1990.
* Out of print. • Temporarily out of print.